Guide to Customer Surveys

Sample questionnaires

and detailed guidelines

for creating effective surveys

Written by
Trevor M. Spunt
Hepworth + Company Ltd.

Published by
The Customer Service Group
215 Park Avenue South, Suite 1301
New York, NY 10003
(212) 228-0246

ISBN 0-915910-47-0
Library of Congress Catalog Card Number: 99-60830

Contents

About The Author

Trevor M. Spunt is a Senior Consultant with Hepworth + Company Ltd., a consulting firm recognized as a leader in the field of customer retention and loyalty management. During the course of his career, he has actively worked to promote and improve quality customer service in a number of customer service environments across a broad spectrum of industries. As advisor to senior management, he has facilitated the implementation of fully integrated, technology-based customer satisfaction measurement and tracking systems. In his book, Mr. Spunt applies his knowledge and expertise as he explains his six-step approach to questionnaire design.

Mr. Spunt earned his Master of Business Administration, specializing in strategic management and organizational behavior, from York University in Toronto, Canada. He also has a Bachelor of Arts degree (Economics) from York University and a Human Resources Development Certificate from the Ontario Society for Training and Development.

Acknowledgements

Many individuals have played a decisive role in helping me to write this book. I would like to thank Michael Hepworth and Paula Mateus who provided me with many helpful suggestions and ideas; Philip Maynard and Sharon Baker who provided important insights; and Beth Berglund, Erika Van Noort, Tania Meyers and Nancy Clements who have read, reviewed and commented on portions of the text. I would also like to thank Susan Hash of The Customer Service Group for her editorial suggestions.

Finally, I wish to thank all those who have contributed to the book by submitting their questionnaires for inclusion. Although we were unable to include all the questionnaires that were submitted, valuable insights were gained which added to the overall quality of this book.

This book is dedicated to the memory of Stanley Spunt and Steve Ramlochan, my greatest teachers.

Foreword

In one of the Pink Panther films, Inspector Clouseau, played by Peter Sellers, asks, "Does your dog bite?" When told the answer is no, he attempts to pat the dog and is promptly bitten. The unfortunate Clouseau says, "I thought you said your dog doesn't bite?" whereupon he is told: "That is not my dog."

What has this got to do with customer questionnaires? The answer is quite simple. You can ask anything you like in a questionnaire but the answers you get may not lead you in the direction you need to go. This applies equally to question structure as it does to question content and to overall questionnaire design.

There is often a feeling among non-researchers that, because we think we know what we want to find out, it is a simple matter of writing questions, putting them in a questionnaire format and asking customers to answer them. What is often overlooked is the depth of knowledge and the process required in developing a professional and effective questionnaire. Like so many subjects, you only discover that you don't know what you don't know once you begin to investigate the issue at deeper levels. It is with this in mind that this book was written.

The purpose of this book is to help customer service professionals develop more effective customer satisfaction questionnaires. This book will also be of value as a tool to evaluate the work of those people who may provide your organization with questionnaires. In addition to developing the questionnaire, the process by which you come to design the questionnaire and the way the questionnaire is implemented in the field is every bit as critical as the questionnaire design process itself. Although this book highlights some of these important issues, it is a good idea if you have the option, to have a customer satisfaction research professional review your questionnaire once it has been developed.

The focus of this book is on surveying external customers. However much of what is done with external customers also relates to internal customers. Thus, if your mandate is surveying internal customers, almost everything covered in this book is relevant to your needs as well.

In compiling the book, we reviewed hundreds of questionnaires used by companies both large and small and in many different industries in our quest to provide you with examples of good questionnaire design. Many of those reviewed had several excellent features, but the vast majority of the questionnaires submitted included design flaws ranging from minor to quite severe. Our purpose was not to find fault but to find good material to use as positive examples in the book. As a result, references to questionnaires focus on the positive aspects of the questionnaires themselves. We would like to take this opportunity to thank all those people who so readily volunteered their questionnaires for inclusion in the book. We apologize to those who went to the trouble of submitting material that did not find its way into the book.

In terms of the layout of the book, the first chapter provides a thorough discussion of the core elements of questionnaire design. The criteria for good questionnaire design discussed in this chapter were used to select the questionnaires to be included in this book. The remaining chapters focus on the three most common types of customer satisfaction questionnaires (recent transactions, overall satisfaction and product/process improvement). Although there is some overlap in questionnaire content between chapters, there are unique aspects to each questionnaire type, aspects which will be discussed within each chapter.

Lastly, we would like to strongly encourage dialogue from users of this book. Our experience is that we also learn from the questions we get asked. We wish you every success in your surveying efforts and hope the knowledge that you gain from reading this book will help you to build long and profitable relationships with your customers.

Michael Hepworth
President
Hepworth + Company

Chapter 1

Designing the Questionnaire

In this age of fierce competition, as evidenced by the seemingly endless reports of mergers, deregulation and global expansion, maintaining a company's competitiveness is becoming an increasingly difficult task. Companies are expanding and businesses are responding by providing better, faster and cheaper products and services in their efforts to maintain and increase market share.

As companies produce products and services that are more appealing to their customers, the industry benchmark, the "standard" of customer expectations, rises. The introduction of the Japanese automobile to North America and the implementation of protective seals on Tylenol bottles by Johnson & Johnson are prime examples of initiatives that heightened customer expectations within these industries.

Rising customer expectations coupled with the proliferation of companies offering similar products and services means that customers have greater choice, and can be more selective of the firms with which they choose to do business. To survive, a firm must learn how to retain its customers. And doing so requires a thorough understanding of their customer's needs and expectations. However, this in itself is not enough. Companies must also be able to incorporate this information into their business strategies and take the necessary action to protect their customer base. Only then will they be poised to create sustained customer loyalty toward their organization.

The tool that bridges this gap between a customer's actual needs and expectations and a company's knowledge of them is the customer satisfaction questionnaire. It is this tool that provides companies with the information necessary both to fulfill the expectations of existing customers and anticipate the needs of future ones.

The Customer Satisfaction Questionnaire

A customer satisfaction questionnaire is a tool that, if designed properly, is able to accurately measure the perceptions and experiences of customers. You will note that we use the term *questionnaire* and not *survey* in describing this data-gathering tool. To do otherwise would be misleading as a survey is not a questionnaire but a process that encompasses the use of an instrument commonly referred to as a questionnaire.

The survey process itself involves defining what you wish to measure (your objectives), the group of people who you wish to survey (the population), the number of people within the group who you wish to survey (the sample), the medium used to survey these people (mail, telephone, Internet, etc.) and the survey instrument itself (the questionnaire). To thoroughly address all these aspects of the survey process is outside the scope of this book and to do so would detract from our main objective of providing you with practical advice on questionnaire design. However, good questionnaire design does require a basic understanding of these areas and, for this reason, they will be briefly discussed. For a more extensive discussion of these issues, read Jon Anton's book, *Listening to the Voice of the Customer*.

The Essentials of Good Questionnaire Design

Designing a questionnaire is a more involved process than simply creating a set of questions for your customers to answer. Many people think if they know how to ask a question, they know how to design a questionnaire. However, proper questionnaire design requires taking into account a number of issues. They include:

1. Setting your objectives*

2. Choosing your target audience*

3. Determining your survey medium *

4. Constructing your questionnaire

5. Conducting your survey

6. Analyzing and reporting the results

* Must be completed prior to the questionnaire constructing.

Each are discussed below.

1. Setting your objectives

The first step in any customer satisfaction measurement project is determining the purpose of your study. Often organizations embark on a customer service improvement project without a clear action plan or objective(s). This results in confusion later on in the project, unnecessary delays and lack of "buy-in" by key organizational decision-makers. To overcome this, adequate planning is essential.

In planning to conduct research with their customers, questionnaire designers need to be clear about the following issues:

- What is your overall goal?
  - To improve customer satisfaction?
  - To improve service quality?
  - To improve customer value?
  - To understand the key "Points of Pain" in certain key transactions?
- What will be done with the data you collect?
- What decisions will be impacted as a result of the findings?
- How will the data be reported and to whom?
- How will you know if you are collecting the right data?
- Who will be responsible for acting on the data?
- How will various sources of information be linked?

The outcome of this planning activity should be the development of the critical elements to the project, agreement on final deliverables and responsibilities for all those involved.

2. Choosing your target audience

In addition to setting the overall objectives for your survey, you must also determine which of your customers you wish to survey. In other words, what are the characteristics of your population? If you wish to solicit suggestions for improvement, you many want to survey those who either have dealt with your company and/or experienced a problem in the recent past.

Surveying people who have not had contact with your product or service may be of some value in market research, but will be of little value in gauging satisfaction with your particular product or service. Surveying such people will also compromise the reliability of your results as any responses from those who have had no exposure to your product and service will likely be random and thus bias your results.

Another consideration is the wording and phrases used in your questionnaire construction. The language should depend partially on your target audience. For instance, if your audience consists of people who work in a particular industry, acronyms common to the industry should be used. If the questionnaire does not contain these words, respondents may question the relevance of the survey itself, resulting in a lower response rate.

3. Determining your survey medium

Once you know the aspects of customer service that you are going to measure and the characteristics of the respondents you will be surveying, you must determine the method you will use to actually conduct the survey.

There are two types of surveys, interviewer-administered (those conducted via telephone or in-person) and self-administered surveys (those conducted by mail, the Internet or postcard). Following are the advantages and disadvantages to these methods.

Interviewer-administered surveys

You can obtain significant advantages by using a well-trained interviewer to gather the answers to your questions (Warwick, Lininger, 1975). These advantages are as follows:

- A permissive atmosphere is created for discussion, which increases the likelihood that your customer will provide complete answers.

- An opportunity for asking questions and clarifying answers is created. Unlike self-administered surveys, it is not dependent on the literacy, educational level or visual acuity of your customer.

- Control over the sequence of the questions, completion of all questions and other aspects of the data-gathering process is ensured. One problem with self-administered surveys is that your customers have the opportunity to scan the questions as they wish. This creates a potential response bias in that the questions and answers of future questions may negatively impact responses provided on previous ones.

Despite these advantages, using an interviewer can be costly, particularly in the case of in-person interviews where travel and associated costs are often involved.

Self-administered surveys

There are also significant advantages to using self-administered surveys.

- They are typically less expensive to administer than the interviewer-administered survey.

- The possibility of interviewer bias is eliminated because customers are insulated from the expectations of the interviewer.

- They allow your customers privacy in answering questions which reduces the likelihood of the social desirability response bias, particularly if respondents consider some of the questions to be threatening or offensive.

- The probability of reaching your customers is greater because you are not dependent on their availability to speak with the interviewer.

- They allow for a large number of customers to be surveyed in a shorter time.

- The results can be obtained more quickly, particularly if the Internet is used.

A note regarding the Internet...

The likelihood that the population of customers you wish to survey via the Internet (a) have the necessary access to respond to your questionnaire and (b) are prepared to use this medium for this purpose is small. Nevertheless, our experience has shown that these barriers are becoming less of an issue as Internet use continues to grow. With the number of Internet users estimated to reach 200 million by the end of the year 2000, it will become an increasingly viable survey methodology.

4. Constructing your questionnaire: The six elements of questionnaire design

As discussed earlier, the questionnaire is your survey tool. The care you take in constructing your questionnaire will impact the response rate of your study, as well as the reliability and validity of your results.

What follows are the six essential elements of questionnaire design. Elements one to five are presented in order of increasing granularity, whereas the last element, Questionnaire Reliability and Validity, refers to the integrity of the questionnaire overall. Within each of these elements are suggestions to aid you in the production of an effective questionnaire.

A. Questionnaire Layout

The visual appearance of the questionnaire.

B. Questionnaire Content

The items to be included in the questionnaire.

C. Questionnaire Flow

The order of the questions and the overall continuity of the questionnaire.

D. Question Structure

The various characteristics of the questions and their corresponding response sets.

E. Question Wording

The wording of the questions and response sets.

F. Questionnaire Reliability and Validity

The factors that affect the reliability and validity of the questionnaire results.

In some cases, a given criterion will be applicable to all five types of questionnaires (mail, Internet, postcard, telephone and in-person). In other cases, it may only be applicable to some of the questionnaire types. The following icons will be used to indicate the survey medium(s) to which each criterion applies.

Mail	✉	Telephone	☎
Internet	WWW	In-person	🧍
Postcard	PC □		

A. Questionnaire Layout

Questionnaires should be visually appealing ✉ WWW PC ☎*

Visual appeal can have a direct impact on your customer's willingness to complete your questionnaire. If your customer feels that it is too complex, difficult to read or difficult to follow, the likelihood that he or she will complete it is lessened. If the questionnaire is returned incomplete, it will bias your results or be rejected. The appearance can also affect the response rate. To avoid these problems, it is best to aim at a relatively conservative but pleasant appearance for your questionnaire (Oppenheim, 1992). Chapters 2-4 provide many examples of questionnaires that do just that.

Questionnaires should not exceed 5-8 pages ✉ WWW PC 🧍☎*

An excessively long questionnaire is demanding on your customers. If your questionnaire exceeds a range of five to eight pages, you must ask yourself if it is asking the right questions. It is possible that the questionnaire is unnecessarily burdening your customer with questions that provide no real value to the study.

With in-person and telephone interviews, questionnaire length can generally be longer than with mail, Internet or postcard because the primary objective isn't appearance, but the ease with which the interviewer can move through the questionnaire. These questionnaires may also require space for notations that will extend the questionnaire's length.

In all cases, it is best to pre-test the questionnaire with a small sample of customers (five to 10) to ensure that the length is appropriate for your study.

The Questionnaire should be interesting ✉ WWW PC 🧍☎

It is important that your questionnaire be visually appealing, and that the content be interesting to your customer. Customers who see value in, and get some enjoyment from, responding to the questionnaire are more likely to do so.

Furthermore, the questionnaire should be viewed as not only a chance to solicit information from your customer, but also as an opportunity to create a positive impression of your company. It is a essentially a direct-mail piece and should be treated as such.

---

* In the case of professionally conducted telephone interviewing, a CATI (computer-assisted telephone interview) is typically used. This negates the impact of visual appeal from a questionnaire design perspective as the software controls the actual display of the questions. However, for those who engage in telephone interviewing using a paper format, this criterion will still apply.

B. Questionnaire Content

A Pre-Survey letter should be included ✉ ☎ WWW

A Pre-Survey letter informs your customer that a questionnaire will be arriving or phone call will be received in the near future and requests their participation in the study. Sending this type of letter introduces your questionnaire to your customers, and through doing so, increases their willingness to participate, which increases your response rate. In the case of Internet surveys, some firms may elect to use email as the medium for communicating the pre-survey message.

Include a cover letter or memo ✉ WWW

A cover letter or memo should be included to introduce the questionnaire to your customer. Ideally, you should personalize it by using your customer's name. In the content of the memo, explain your company's reason for choosing him or her to participate in the survey. Be sure to explain that their participation will ultimately benefit them as well (Berdie, 1986). Examples of cover letters and memos can be found in Chapters 2-4.

Include your company's name and address on the questionnaire ✉ PC

Make sure the name and address to where the completed questionnaire should be sent appears on the questionnaire, and in the case of mail questionnaires, on the self-addressed return envelope. Doing so reduces the impact on your response rate should the envelope and questionnaire get separated.

Refrain from asking 'nice to know' questions ✉ WWW PC ☎

Questionnaire designers are sometimes tempted to adopt the "while you are out there" approach and ask questions that aren't directly pertinent to the study objectives. By doing so, two problems emerge. First, the flow of the questionnaire may be compromised as customers address unrelated topics. Second, it unnecessarily increases the length of the survey. This can erode your response rate if the questionnaire is found to be too cumbersome to complete.

Keep in mind, a questionnaire that is only partially completed is worthless to your company and, in the case of telephone interviews, time-consuming, costly and frustrating to the interviewer and your customer.

C. Questionnaire Flow

The questionnaire should be logical

Questionnaire designers must ensure that the questions flow logically into each other and, ideally, in the order in which your customer is exposed to a situation with your company. Questions that are unrelated or appear to have no relevance from the customer's perspective run the risk of being left unanswered. And with mail, Internet or postcard questionnaires it may trigger frustration, which can quickly lead to respondent fatigue and result in a questionnaire that is only partially completed or discarded.

Interesting and/or most important questions should appear at the beginning

The first question is the most crucial one. It determines whether or not the questionnaire is going to be completed. With this in mind, characteristics of the first questions should be as follows:

- It should be clearly related to the objectives of your study.

- It should be easily understood and answered (it should not be an open-ended question*).

- It should be neutral. Questions that ask your customers to state whether or not they agree with a particular issue should be avoided.

- It should be a question of interest to all your customers.

* for an explanation of this term, refer to page 13

Skip patterns should be clearly indicated

When skip patterns are used (a request to skip to a question other than the next one in the questionnaire), they should appear right beside the actual response. For example:

9. Have you contacted ABC in the past 12 months?

   1. YES ○   (CONTINUE TO THE NEXT QUESTION)

   2. NO ○   (GO TO QUESTION 14)

Skip patterns should be minimal

Although questionnaires may require that skip patterns be used, it is best to do so sparingly, as they can easily lead to confusion. Furthermore, excessive use of skip patterns may lead customers to believe that the questionnaire wasn't constructed with them in mind, especially if they're asked to skip over too many sets of questions as they proceed through it.

Questions should not be split between two pages

Make an effort to keep a question and its corresponding response set (the set of responses from which your customer may choose) on the same page (Dillman, 1978). Forcing your customer to turn a page in the middle of a question will create confusion. It may also lead to errors if your customer doesn't accurately transcribe the rating scales to the next page. Techniques for avoiding split questions include re-arranging question order slightly or manipulating spacing in the question.

If you are using an items-in-a-series style question (a question which measures attributes using a common rating scale), it may be necessary to continue onto a new page. In this case, be sure that the new page appears opposite the existing one as opposed to on the back of the questionnaire.

Less objectionable questions should appear  before more objectionable ones

If questions are included that could be considered intrusive, it is best to place them near the end of the questionnaire in order to avoid premature termination of the questionnaire.

Demographic questions should be placed  near the end of the questionnaire

Demographic questions are those that measure what people are, for example, those which are related to age, gender, education and occupation. Because some demographic questions can be considered intrusive, it is best to place them at the end of the questionnaire unless they are required for screening purposes.

Questions should be relevant

A question is relevant if your customer considers the question to be of value in the context of answering the questionnaire. If customers begin to complete a question and find that their response, in their opinion, will be of little value, there is a strong likelihood that they will terminate the questionnaire. Therefore, it is important to begin the questionnaire by asking questions that are relevant to your customers. For example, if you are measuring your customer's level of satisfaction with a product that they regularly purchase from you, and you are a producer of many products, a relevant question might be: "Which of these products have you purchased from us in the past year?" It is deemed relevant because your customer can easily see the connection between the question and the purpose of the questionnaire (which should have been explained in your memo or cover letter for self-administered questionnaires and by the interviewer for interviewer-administered questionnaires).

Questions with similar themes should be grouped together

This rule applies not only to questions that are similar in content, but also to those which are similar in structure. For example, if you ask a series of questions about an experience at a restaurant, questions relating to the staff (being greeted at the door, attentiveness, knowledge of the menu) would appear in one section on the questionnaire, whereas questions about the food (taste, menu variety, temperature) would appear in a separate section. Within each of these sections, the question types used to ask these questions would also be grouped together.

The reasons for grouping questions in this way are two-fold:

1. The mental effort required to switch between question types is lessened.

2. Your customers are more likely to provide well-thought-out answers if the questions asked appear in an order that is logical to them.

D. Question Structure

Use lowercase type for questions, uppercase type for responses

Your customers will be able to complete the questionnaire more easily if you provide different case types for questions and answers. Case type is a useful way of keeping customers on track because it is subtle and doesn't interfere with the task at hand. Lowercase type is used for questions and uppercase for responses — and not vice versa — because lowercase is typically easier to read than uppercase. Also, since questions are usually longer than their response set, it is wise to use lowercase type for the questions (Dillman, 1978).

Response sets should be vertically aligned

Response sets and their corresponding numbers should be arranged vertically on the page (see example below). There are several reasons for doing so (Dillman, 1978):

- It prevents the possibility of omitting answers to questions, which can occur if your customers are required to move back and forth across the pages to answer questions.

- It eliminates the possibility of incorrectly marking the wrong side of the response.

- It creates a sense of accomplishment as your customers move down the page.

- It creates significant white space on the page, which makes it easier to complete the questionnaire.

INCORRECT

1) How did you obtain the XXX Customer Service phone number?

WHITE PAGES   AN ADVERTISEMENT   A PRODUCT BROCHURE   EMAIL

2) Did you speak to a medical information expert about your issue?

YES   NO   DON'T KNOW

3) How many times were you transferred before reaching someone who could help you?

NOT TRANSFERRED   1   2   3   4   5   6

CORRECT

1) How did you obtain the ABC Customer Service phone number?

    A) WHITE PAGES   ○

    B) AN ADVERTISEMENT   ○

    C) A PRODUCT BROCHURE   ○

    D) EMAIL   ○

2) Did you speak to a medical information expert about your issue?

    A) YES   ○

    B) NO   ○

    C) DON'T KNOW   ○

3) How many times were you transferred before reaching someone who could help you?

    A) NOT TRANSFERRED   ○

    B) 1   ○

    C) 2   ○

    D) 3   ○

    E) 4   ○

    F) 5   ○

    G) 6   ○

    H) 7+   ○

Provide directions on how to answer questions

Asking a question and providing a set of responses does not automatically result in the required response from your customer. Experience has shown that customers will resort to various types of markings (checkmarks, lines, Xs) while completing self-administered questionnaires. This creates ambiguity for the coder and, in the case of pre-coded questionnaires, unanswered questions. To prevent this, directions must be provided (Dillman, 1978).

Although it may appear excessive to provide directions for each question, it is better to overexplain than take the chance that questions will be incorrectly marked.

Directions can be differentiated from the questions through the use of brackets as shown in the following example:

What is your primary method of contact with ABC? **(PLEASE CHECK ONE)**

1. TELEPHONE	○	4. EMAIL	○
2. LETTER	○	5. INTERNET	○
3. IN PERSON	○	6. FAX	○

For series questions, use dots to join the attribute to the rating scale

A common question type is the items-in-a-series style question. This question is used when you wish to rate several attributes using the same rating scale. When using this type of format, keep in mind that the accuracy of responses may be compromised if your customers fail to rate the attribute using the scale that is provided beside it. To avoid this, it is best to add a series of dots between the question and the corresponding rating scale. An example is shown below.

10) Now I'd like to ask you to rate how satisfied you were with the service provided by the XXX customer service people. For each statement I read, please tell me whether you were:

	Very Satisfied	Satisfied	Neither Satisfied Nor Dissatisfied	Dissatisfied	Very Dissatisfied	Don't know/ Not Applicable
Representative who responded to your question/issue						
1. Professional/courteous	❏	❏	❏	❏	❏	❏
2. Concern about your question/issue	❏	❏	❏	❏	❏	❏
3. Willing to help you	❏	❏	❏	❏	❏	❏
4. Knowledgeable about your question/ issue	❏	❏	❏	❏	❏	❏
5. Had authority to resolve your question/ issue	❏	❏	❏	❏	❏	❏
6. Followed through on actions she/he promised to take	❏	❏	❏	❏	❏	❏
7. Accuracy of the information provided	❏	❏	❏	❏	❏	❏
8. Overall how satisfied were you with your experience contacting XXX customer service?	❏	❏	❏	❏	❏	❏

Proper question types should be used ✉ WWW PC 人 ☎

There are four types of questions you can use to solicit information from your customers: open-ended questions, closed-ended questions with ordered responses, closed-ended questions with unordered responses and partially closed-ended questions (Dillman, 1978). Each type has its own set of characteristics and is suitable for different situations. Each are explained below.

a) Open-ended question

This type of question is used when the number of possibilities that your customers could provide is too large to be contained within a response set or the possibilities themselves are unknown. For example:

Do you have any suggestions that would make your contact experience with the company more effective? _____

_____

_____

_____

_____

Advantages

• Great for exploratory or qualitative research to prepare for the development of closed-ended questions in a later questionnaire.

• Used to stimulate free thought, solicit suggestions and probe customers' memories.

Disadvantages

• It is onerous on the interviewee.

• Illegible handwriting can present a problem (applies to mail and postcard questionnaires only).

• Poses difficulties for statistical analysis because the responses must first be subjectively interpreted.

b) Closed-ended question with ordered responses

In this type of question, your customers are free to answer along a single dimension of some concept, as illustrated in the following example. The concept is satisfaction and the dimension is the degree to which your customers are satisfied.

Overall, how satisfied are you with ABC as a pharmaceutical company? Are you...

(READ LIST)

1. VERY SATISFIED	○
2. SATISFIED	○
3. NEITHER SATISFIED NOR DISSATISFIED	○
4. DISSATISFIED	○
5. VERY DISSATISFIED	○

Advantages

- Effective for determining intensity of feeling, degree of involvement and frequency of participation.

- Only appropriate when you have a well-defined issue and know precisely what dimension of thought you want your customers to use when providing their answer.

- Typically less demanding than other question types.

c) Closed-ended question with unordered choices

The difference between this question type and closed-ended with ordered choices is that the responses do not limit customers to choosing along a single continuum. An example of this type of question is illustrated below.

Please indicate which one of the following amusement rides was the least enjoyable?

1. JUMBO KING	○
2. PETER'S PALACE	○
3. THE DRAGON DUNGEON	○

Advantages

- Effective in establishing priorities among issues.

- Useful for evaluating individually each alternative against the others.

Disadvantages

- More difficult to answer in telephone interviews because it requires your customers to balance several ideas concurrently.

- Unless you have sufficient knowledge of the subject to create meaningful answer choices (usually by conducting a focus group with a small number of customers), useful results cannot be obtained.

d) Partially close-ended question

This question type was developed for situations in which all possible answer choices are not included in the response set. By adding an "other" response, the questionnaire allows your customers an option if the provided responses do not apply. An example of this question type is provided below.

What was the reason for your contact with the company?

A)	TO OBTAIN MEDICAL INFORMATION	○
B)	TO PLACE AN ORDER / REQUEST STATUS OF ORDER	○
C)	TO REQUEST EDUCATIONAL MATERIAL	○
D)	TO FOLLOW UP BASED ON SALES REP INFORMATION	○
E)	TO REQUEST FREE SAMPLES	○
F)	TO COMPLAIN ABOUT THE PRODUCT	○
G)	OTHER_____	○

Advantages

- This eliminates the disadvantage of question type (c) by providing your customers with an opportunity to offer alternate responses.

- It signals a problem of insufficient answer choices if an unusually high number of volunteered choices are provided.

E. Question Wording

The wording of questions is the most critical component of your questionnaire because the questions are your conduit through which the information is gathered. Questions that are not worded correctly can lower your response rate and provide you with results that do not fulfill your study objectives. In extreme cases, if your questions lack focus to the point of being cumbersome to answer, this can lead to a negative impression of your company.

For these reasons, it is important to develop high-quality questions that will be interpreted in the same manner by all readers of your questionnaire, will be perceived to be of value to your customers and will be consistent with your study objectives.

Because the actual wording of your questions will depend largely on the objectives of your study, it is impossible to provide the specific wording for your questions. However, there are general guidelines you can follow.

There are four types of questions that can be asked in a questionnaire, those that measure: 1) attitudes, 2) beliefs, 3) behaviors and 4) demographics (Dillman, 1978). Your study objectives should help you to determine which type of questions to ask.

1. Attitudes

Attitudes are a measure of what your customers want. Asking your customers about their attitudes is asking them to communicate their preferences toward something, in this case, your products and services. Words commonly used to measure attitudes are favor/oppose, prefer/not prefer, should/should not, good/bad, right/wrong and desirable/undesirable.

Here are a few examples of questions that measure attitudes:

a) Which of the following products do you prefer?

b) Do you consider ABC Car Company's decision to put prices on the cars in the showroom a good one?

c) Should abortions be performed at XYZ Hospital?

2. Beliefs

Beliefs are a measure of what people think is true. To get an accurate reflection of your customers' beliefs, avoid implying goodness or badness in the response choices. Words commonly used to measure beliefs are correct/incorrect, accurate/inaccurate, and what happened/what did not happen. The following are examples of questions that measure beliefs.

a) Have you been receiving accurate invoices?

YES   O

NO   O

b) Which ONE of the following statements BEST describes your feelings about the action taken by the Customer Service department to resolve your question/issue?

I WAS COMPLETELY SATISFIED	O
I WAS NOT COMPLETELY SATISFIED, BUT THE ACTION TAKEN WAS ACCEPTABLE	O
I WAS NOT COMPLETELY SATISFIED, BUT SOME ACTION WAS TAKEN	O
I WAS NOT AT ALL SATISFIED WITH THE ACTION TAKEN	O
I WAS NOT AT ALL SATISFIED BECAUSE NO ACTION WAS TAKEN	O

c) What period of time do you consider to be acceptable?

WITHIN 1 HOUR	O
1 OR MORE HOURS BUT LESS THAN 4 HOURS	O
4 OR MORE HOURS BUT LESS THAN 24 HOURS	O
1 OR MORE DAYS BUT LESS THAN 2 DAYS	O
2 OR MORE DAYS BUT LESS THAN 5 DAYS	O
5 OR MORE DAYS	O

3. Behavior

Understanding customer behavior is critical to generating and maintaining customer loyalty. Measuring behavior includes understanding what your customers have done in the past, what they are currently doing and what they are likely to do. Keep in mind that even if you ask your customers what they are likely to do, there is no guarantee that they will actually follow through on what they said they would do. However, research by Hepworth + Company has shown that, if your customers indicate they are "very satisfied" with an aspect of your product or service (a top box/score rating), they will likely repurchase your product or service and recommend it to others. Hepworth research has also found that when customers are less than "very satisfied" with a company, their willingness to repurchase your product or service and recommend it to others drops by more than 30% (Hepworth, 1998). Some questions that measure behavior are:

a) On a 5-point scale where 5 means "definitely would" and 1 means "definitely would not," how likely is it that you would recommend product X to other hospital administrators?

     5   4   3   2   1   **NOT APPLICABLE**

b) On a 5-point scale where 5 means "definitely would" and 1 means "definitely would not," how likely is it that you would choose company X as the supplier of product X for your hospital?

     5   4   3   2   1   **NOT APPLICABLE**

c) Do you feel that you would use this service in the next 3 months?

    1. YES   O

    2. NO   O

    3. NOT SURE   O

4. Demographics

Demographics are a measure of what people are. You can ask demographic questions to gain an understanding of your customers' characteristics, which may reflect how they will answer the attitude, beliefs and behavior questions. Common attribute questions include those related to age, gender, occupation and education. Here are a few examples of demographic questions:

a) Gender:

    1. MALE   O

    2. FEMALE   O

b) What year did you obtain your Medical Degree?

_____

c) Approximately how many prescriptions do you write per month?

1. UP TO 10 ○

2. 11 TO 40 ○

3. 41 TO 80 ○

4. 81 TO 100 ○

5. 101+ ○

By understanding the types of questions that can be used in your questionnaire, and the corresponding information that each type can obtain, you can ensure that the ones you choose will support rather than detract from your efforts to meet your survey objectives.

Questionnaire vocabulary should be simple

It is important that your questions are written with words that are easily understood. Otherwise, the responses provided will not be consistent with what you intended to measure. The only exception would be for questionnaires aimed at customers from a specific industry. For example, if your customers (target audience) were lawyers, and you were providing a service that offered name searches for companies wishing to register their businesses, you could use the term "Articles of Incorporation" (a document filed with the state agency to register the business). In this case, all your customers would be familiar with the term and would expect you to use it. If you had simplified this term by trying to explain the idea in a different way (i.e., official form used to register the business), this may lead your target audience of lawyers to question the knowledge of the company conducting the survey and negatively impact your response rate and customer perceptions.

Again, pre-testing the questionnaire with your target audience is the best way to ensure that your questions are understood.

Questions and/or response sets should not be vague

At first glance, this point may appear rather obvious. However, there have been many occasions in which questionnaires have contained vague questions and response sets that resulted in unusable information.

Two examples of this are provided below. The first is an open-ended question with the question itself being vague. The second is a closed-ended question with the response sets being vague. Both are accompanied by suggested revisions to illustrate the effect that have vague questions and/or response sets can have on questionnaire outcome.

a) **Vague** What changes should be made to our company?

Improved What changes should our company make to improve our service to you?

b) **Vague**   How often did you visit our store in the past year?

                    1. NEVER   O

                    2. RARELY   O

                    3. OCCASIONALLY O

                    4. REGULARLY   O

Improved   How often did you visit our store in the past year?

          1. NOT AT ALL   O

          2. LESS THAN ONCE A MONTH   O

          3. ABOUT ONCE A MONTH   O

          4. ABOUT TWO TO THREE TIMES A MONTH O

          5. ABOUT ONCE A WEEK   O

          6. MORE THAN ONCE A WEEK   O

Questions are not too precise

To avoid being vague, questionnaire designers sometimes end up writing questions that are too precise. How can a question be too precise? After all, the more focused the question, the more likely that what you are measuring is consistent with what you intended to measure. However, consider the following question aimed at a target audience of doctors:

How many prescriptions have you written in the past month?

_____ (NUMBER)

To respond to this question, doctors would need to check their records and calculate an answer. Many doctors would not bother with this time-consuming task, and some might resent the expectation that they provide an accurate answer. A better version of the question would be:

How many prescriptions have you written in the past year?

    1. NONE   O

    2. 1 TO 250   O

    3. 251 TO 500   O

    4. 501 TO 751   O

    5. 751 TO 1,000 O

    6. 1,000+   O

Asking the question in this manner allows the doctor to provide an answer that is likely sufficient for your study without requiring excessive effort on their part.

Questions are not offensive

There are several reasons why your customers may consider a question to be offensive. A primary reason is that they believe the question is requesting personal information, such as asking your customer to state their annual income. The best way to deal with these types of questions is to change the question from a direct one to one that uses broad categories.

Narrow → Broad

Narrow   What is your annual income?

_____ (Dollars)

Broad   Which of the following categories best describes your annual income?

1. LESS THAN $10,000   ○

2. $10,000 TO $25,000   ○

3. $25,001 TO $40,000   ○

4. $40,001 TO $55,000   ○

5. $55,001 TO $70,000   ○

6. $70,001+   ○

Questions that consider the element of time

When asking questions that measure customer activity during a specific time period, be sure to take into account behavior that is inherently cyclical. For example, consider the situation where a bank asks its customers the following question:

Have you made your retirement savings plan contribution for the 1998 tax year?

Yes   ○

No   ○

If you ask this question over a three-month period, the responses can differ significantly depending on the actual date that the customer completes the questionnaire. For instance, a customer who completes the questionnaire in January is more likely to indicate "No" compared to a customer who fills out the questionnaire in April. It is thus important to consider the survey period when asking questions that may be influenced by cycles of behavior, otherwise, biases can occur.

F. Questionnaire Reliability and Validity

It is common to confuse reliability with validity. To clarify these terms: Reliability refers to the questionnaire's ability to provide the same feedback from customers regardless of which random sample of customers you choose to survey whereas validity refers to your ability to construct a questionnaire that will give you the information that you intended to obtain.

For example, it is possible for you to reliably determine that customers are satisfied with the overall quality of product X by conducting numerous surveys of different samples of your customer population. But, if the survey objective was to determine whether or not customers were happy with specific aspects of their experience with your company related to the purchase of product X, the results may be reliable but not necessarily valid for your specific purposes.

As the determination of questionnaire validity is specific to your survey objectives, it is difficult to provide you with criteria to ensure that it is valid other than the suggestion already discussed of pre-testing the questionnaire with target audience. As such, this section will concentrate on issues that can negatively impact questionnaire reliability.

There should be no leading questions

Leading questions inherently influence your customers to answer questions in a particular way. This can result in biased responses. Consider the following example:

Many of our customers are very satisfied with quality of product X? How do you feel?

    I agree   O

    I disagree   O

This question will result in a greater number of your customers answering "I agree" because they are being asked to support a positive statement rather than provide their opinion on an issue. A better way to obtain the same information would be:

How satisfied are you with the quality of product X?

    Very Satisfied   O

    Satisfied   O

    Neither Satisfied nor Dissatisfied   O

    Dissatisfied   O

    Very Dissatisfied   O

Asking the question in this manner keeps it neutral, which will give you a more reliable response.

Questions should be uni-dimensional

Uni-dimensional questions limit measurement to one element of customer perception. When companies are measuring several aspects of customer satisfaction, more than one element may be incorporated into the same question. However, doing so will taint the results because there's no way to determine which element you are actually measuring. Consider the wording of the following question:

Do you find our sales representatives to be friendly and knowledgeable?

Yes   O

No   O

This question could actually be interpreted in a number of ways. Are your sales representatives friendly? Are your sales representatives knowledgeable? Are your sales representatives friendly and knowledgeable?

As a result, there's no way to find out how the question is truly being perceived and, thus, how to interpret the actual responses. A better way of handling this type of question is to split it into single, distinct ideas:

Please rate our sales representatives on the following attributes. Are they ...

	Yes	No
Friendly	O	O
Knowledgeable	O	O

Writing the question in this manner will enable you to ensure that what you intend to measure is congruent with what you are actually measuring.

Responses should be mutually exclusive

When writing questions that involve ranges such as those related to income, be careful to ensure that all response sets do not overlap. Consider the following question.

Please indicate your annual income:

$15,000 OR LESS	O
$15,000 TO $30,000	O
$30,000 TO $45,000	O
$45,000 TO $60,000	O
$60,000 TO $75,000	O
$75,000+	O

If one of your customers were to receive an annual income of, for example, $30,000, they would have difficulty determining which of the two ranges to choose. To correct this problem, rewrite the question as follows:

Please indicate your annual income:

$15,000 OR LESS	○
$15,001 TO $30,000	○
$30,001 TO $45,000	○
$45,001 TO $60,000	○
$60,001 TO $75,000	○
$75,001+	○

Questions should not contain a behavioral expectation bias

The term behavioral expectation refers to the expectation that your customer will respond to a question in a certain way in order to conform to what is expected or "fit in." In the question below, your customer is being told that the majority of customers have purchased a product within the recent past and is being asked if they have done so as well.

Most customers have purchased brand X in the past 3 months, have you?

Yes	○
No	○

Asking a question in this way may create a social desirability response in your customers and inappropriately influence the outcome of the answer. A social desirability response is an action taken by someone in their effort to conform to what they believe would be "acceptable" by others. With this in mind, a better way to construct the question would be to eliminate the first part of the question:

Have you purchased brand X in the past 3 months?

Yes	○
No	○

Questions should not contain a recall bias

This type of bias can occur because, since memories do not perfectly record events that happen, customers may guess their answers and, in some cases, avoid answering questions altogether. For these reasons, it is important that you design your questionnaire to minimize the effect of this problem. Strategies for doing so include shortening the recall period and/or providing an exhaustive list in your response set to trigger associations for your customer.

Questions are accurate ✉ WWW PC 🧍 ☎

Questions often provide information in addition to asking for it (Dillman, 1978). For this reason, it is important that any questions that contain facts be accurate. It only requires one of your customers to identify a flaw in your questionnaire to discredit the questionnaire and lead them to terminate the questionnaire and lower your response rate. Your questionnaire is also a moment of truth with your customers. If it's flawed, it can also negatively impact the overall impression that your customer has of your company.

5. Conducting Your Survey

There are three important considerations related to the actual collection of information from your customers. First, when conducting your survey, it is important to make sure that the target customers are the ones who complete the questionnaires. Second, a sufficient sample (number of completed questionnaires) must be obtained to conduct the required analysis. If the sample size is insufficient, it will be difficult to draw statistically reliable conclusions from your customer's responses. Finally, in most cases, with the exception of the simplest surveys, completed questionnaires must be coded (assisgning numbers to various responses) in order to conduct this analysis. Doing so reduces the likelihood of data entry errors. For a more detailed discussion of these aspects of survey design, consult Jon Anton's book, *Listening to the Voice of the Customer*.

6. Analyzing and Reporting the Results

When analyzing the data, keep in mind that most of your customers are satisfied with your products and services or they wouldn't continue to do business with you. Your efforts are thus best concentrated on the issues that create dissatisfaction rather than trying to incrementally improve those that currently provide satisfaction.

In terms of actually reporting the results, you may encounter resistance from management to these results. This can occur for a variety of reasons. The chart on page 25 indicates some of those reasons and possible causes.

These are some of the obstacles that can prevent you from using the data you generate to improve your customer satisfaction. The best preventive remedy is proper planning at the initial stage of the project via a management meeting that involves all stakeholders in the study.

Reasons	Causes
Managers do not want to use it	• No ownership • Conflicts with current paradigms • No positive reinforcement for acting on the data • Perceptions of inaccuracy
Managers do not know how to use it	• Information is too "high level" to be meaningful or useful • Information is too complex
Managers do not know what is expected	• Not linked to a strategic or operating plan • Exhibits unclear/unrealistic implementation targets
Internal Barriers	• Conflicting priorities • Internal politics • Lack of effective cross-functional processes

A final word...

By now, it should be clear that questionnaire design is more complex than putting together a set of questions for your customers to answer. It is a task that involves diligent and careful planning in all elements of its design.

What follows are actual questionnaires used by companies across North America that exhibit the questionnaire design elements discussed in this chapter. These questionnaires are examples only rather than templates to be copied without consideration of the validity of the questionnaires themselves to your study. Each of the following chapters represents a particular questionnaire group (recent transactions, product/process improvement, overall satisfaction). Each chapter begins with a discussion of the purpose, characteristics, benefits, and pitfalls of employing this style of questionnaire. Whereas this chapter focused on providing you with practical information on questionnaire design, the main focus of Chapters 2-4 is to provide you with a wide array of sample questionnaires that illustrate the principles of this chapter.

As all of the design elements discussed in this chapter are not present in every questionnaire (if they were, there would be no need for this book), there was a clear need to identify the strengths and weaknesses of each questionnaire. In this regard, a chart has been created immediately prior to each set of questionnaires that identifies their strengths in terms of the six elements of questionnaire design discussed in this chapter. This will help you to quickly identify their strengths in your quest to design a questionnaire that is congruent with your company's objectives, inviting to your customers and a reliable, valid and rich source of information.

Chapter 2

Recent Customer Transaction Questionnaires

Before deciding on which type of questionnaire to use (recent customer transaction, process/product improvement, overall customer satisfaction), it is important first to determine if you wish to use a transactional- or relationship-oriented questionnaire.

Transactional-oriented questionnaires are those that measure customer satisfaction based on a particular transaction, whereas relationship-oriented questionnaires are more concerned with customer satisfaction based on the overall service relationship. Transactional questionnaires are also typically used when a company finds that they are creating many points of pain for their customers within their cycle of service and wish to track their success in eliminating these points of pain. This chapter continues with a discussion of a type of transactional questionnaire that focuses on recent transactions. Relationship-oriented questionnaires can be found in Chapters 3 and 4.

- Are my customers' transactions complex and infrequent? If they are, you will want to consider using a recent transaction questionnaire such as those shown in this chapter. Examples of such transactions would involve taking out a mortgage, or the purchase of a house, automobile, or boat.

- Do I service my customers frequently with simple transactions? Do I know how to contact my customers? If you can answer both of these questions in the affirmative, you probably want to consider a relationship-oriented approach. Banking is one industry that lends itself to a relationship questionnaire.

- Is my ongoing relationship with my customers more important than any individual transaction? If it is, a relationship approach is in order.

There are instances when you will want to consider taking both approaches. This can be done within a single questionnaire by asking about both the latest transaction and the relationship. In this case, the **overall customer satisfaction questionnaire** in Chapter 4 is typically used.

Purpose

Recent transaction questionnaires are used to collect information related to a specific contact experience your customer has had with your company.

Because customers' experiences shape their attitudes, which ultimately determine their behavior, it is important to understand these experiences so that action can be taken to correct the behaviors and processes within the firm that led to these negative experiences. Only then will firms be able to truly benefit from this type of customer satisfaction measurement.

Characteristics

- The questionnaire contains a preamble that asks customers to consider a recent transaction when answering the questionnaire.

- The questionnaire "walks" customers through the full cycle of service by asking questions related to each point of contact with the firm. Each of these "moments of truth" has the potential to negatively or positively impact your customer's attitude toward your firm.

- Questions are predominantly closed-ended.

Pitfalls

The factor most critical to the success or failure of recent customer transaction implementation is that of time. This is broken down into two dimensions: frequency (how frequently your customers are surveyed) and timing (the time between the transaction itself and receipt of the questionnaire).

Frequency

Every time your company name is communicated to your customers, you provide your customers with an opportunity to form an impression of your company. This impression will either be positive, negative or neutral and it will be dependent on factors that are both within and outside your control.

To the extent that you do have control over these impressions, the frequency with which surveys are conducted can directly impact customer perception. If your customers feel they are being excessively surveyed, not only will it create a negative impression of your company, but your customers will likely fail to complete the questionnaire. For these reasons, it is best not to survey any customer more than once every six months. In cases where your survey program is automated to send a questionnaire upon completion of a transaction (as is typically the case of car dealership service centers), it is important that the program be modified to take this issue into account.

Timing

Timing is also an important consideration. If customers are surveyed too soon or too long after their transaction with the firm, problems will arise that affect the reliability of the responses. The two problems that can occur are the Halo Effect and Recall Effect.

Halo Effect

The Halo Effect occurs when your customer has an inflated perception of your product and/or service due to the fact that it has recently been purchased (such as the purchase of a new car) rather than due to the quality of the product or service itself. Believing otherwise would only create stress for the customer, as it may infer a poor purchasing decision on their part.

This effect poses a problem for firms that are so eager to survey their customers that they send the questionnaires too soon after the transaction has been completed. By doing so, firms may not be able to gauge true perceptions of a customer experience, particularly as they relate to product quality. We have also found that as the perceived value of the product increases, the likelihood that this Halo Effect will occur also increases. Although the period immediately following a purchase will differ across companies and products, it is important to consider this issue in a survey process to ensure that your results accurately reflect more grounded customer perceptions.

Recall Effect

In contrast, the Recall Effect can occur if your customers are surveyed too long after the transaction has occurred.

This effect can also occur if there is ambiguity as to which transaction the customer is responding. Examples of this would be banking transactions where transactions are frequent, or credit card transactions where your customers may not be able to differentiate between the experience associated with your card and that of your competitor's card. In these cases, it is important to be able to identify the transaction to which the questionnaire pertains. This could be achieved either through a statement in the cover letter or a statement on the questionnaire itself.

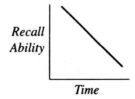

The implication of the Recall Effect is a lower response rate in cases where your customers do not remember the event or are not certain of the event to which you are referring. Customers who do recall the specific event may not recall it in sufficient detail to be able to adequately answer your questionnaire. Those who try may either terminate the questionnaire or provide responses that do not reflect their true experience. That is not to say that this is of no value, as it is their current perception of their experience. However, in order to make effective changes in your organization, it is important that their perception represent a true picture of their experience with your organization.

In addition, erroneous feedback may occur in cases where your customer cannot distinguish between experiences with your company and your competitors and completes your questionnaire based on their collective experiences.

Benefits

> ✓ **An understanding of your customer's perceptions of their transactional experience.**

If your questions are actionable*, you will have sufficient understanding of the weaknesses in your transactional processes to make the necessary changes to improve them.

> ✓ **Opportunity to increase customer loyalty by promptly responding to poor customer evaluations.**

The quick resolution of a customer's issue brings satisfaction, which is likely to translate into loyalty. The Hepworth + Company CustomerPulse™ database shows that in many industries, customers who complain and have their problems resolved satisfactorily are more likely to be loyal than customers who have had no problems at all. If the customer problem is part of a pattern that points to some shortcoming in the company's products or services, corrective action can be taken. The result is improved quality and fewer problems for customers, which increases the likelihood that loyalty will develop. This increased loyalty is reflected in the customer's willingness to buy the product or service again or continue using it; willingness to buy the company's other products; and willingness to recommend the company to others.

What follows are 14 recent transaction questionnaires in various formats (telephone, mail, postcard, Internet) from firms across a broad range of industries. As each of these questionnaires is stronger on some elements of questionnaire design and weaker on others, those that represent strengths in each of the six elements of questionnaire design will be listed in the chart on page 31.

---

* Actionable questions are those that enable you to take action based on the responses your customers provide. A question such as, "Did you have difficulties placing your order?" is not an actionable question, for if your customer responds YES, you do not know what difficulties your customer had. To correct this problem, a follow-up question should be asked requesting your customer to specify the difficulty that they had.

Questionnaire Design Elements	Questionnaire Numbers													
	1	2	3	4	5	6	7	8	9	10	11	12	13	14
Questionnaire Layout	✓	✓	✓	✓	✓		✓	✓	✓		✓	✓	✓	✓
Questionnaire Content				✓	✓		✓	✓	✓	✓	✓	✓	✓	✓
Questionnaire Flow		✓	✓	✓	✓	✓	✓	✓	✓		✓	✓	✓	✓
Questionnaire Structure	✓	✓	✓	✓	✓	✓	✓	✓	✓	✓	✓	✓	✓	✓
Questionnaire Wording	✓	✓	✓	✓	✓	✓	✓	✓	✓	✓	✓	✓	✓	✓
Questionnaire Reliability**	✓	✓	✓	✓			✓	✓	✓	✓	✓	✓	✓	✓

** The ability to assess the validity of a questionnaire is highly dependent on knowing the objective of each survey project. As the objectives specific to your organization will likely be unique, any questionnaires that appear in this box will be based on issues of reliability.

Placing and Receiving Your Order

1. Did you have any difficulties placing your order?
   - ☐ YES
   - ☐ NO

If yes, what would have made it easier?
   - ☐ MORE OR BETTER PRODUCT INFORMATION
   - ☐ CLEARER INSTRUCTIONS ON HOW TO PLACE THE ORDER
   - ☐ MORE HELPFUL SALES REPRESENTATIVE
   - ☐ MORE HELPFUL CUSTOMER RELATIONS REPRESENTATIVE
   - ☐ OTHER _____

2. How would you evaluate the time ABC took to process and deliver your order?
   - ☐ FASTER THAN EXPECTED
   - ☐ ABOUT AS MUCH TIME AS EXPECTED
   - ☐ SLOWER THAN EXPECTED

3. Was the correct ABC product sent?
   - ☐ YES
   - ☐ NO

If yes:
   a. Were any materials missing from the shipment?
   - ☐ YES
   - ☐ NO

   b. Was your order in satisfactory condition?
   - ☐ YES
   - ☐ NO

If no, call Customer Relations: 1-800-222-2222, or give us your comments: _____

4. Were your name and address accurate on the shipping label and packing slip?
   - ☐ YES
   - ☐ NO

(If no, please contact Customer Relations at 1-800-222-2222, or correct the information on the outside of this form prior to mailing.)

ABC's Customer Service

5. Has your ABC Sales Rep contacted you since you received your order?
   - ☐ YES
   - ☐ NO

6. Would you like your ABC Sales Representative to assist you with any of the following?
   - ☐ CHECKING THE ORDER
   - ☐ SETTING UP THE PRODUCT
   - ☐ LEARNING TO USE THE PRODUCT
   - ☐ OTHER _____

7. Have you had any problems installing or using your CD-ROM?
   - ☐ YES
   - ☐ NO

   If yes, please specify: _____

   If yes, has your question been answered or problem resolved to your satisfaction?
   - ☐ YES
   - ☐ NO
   - ☐ DON'T KNOW YET

8. Would you like a ABC CD-ROM Specialist to call you regarding any of the following?
   - ☐ INSTALLING HARDWARE
   - ☐ INSTALLING SOFTWARE
   - ☐ INSTALLING CD-ROM ON A NETWORK
   - ☐ USING/SEARCHING ON CD-ROM
   - ☐ OTHER _____

If yes, please provide your phone number:
( ) _____

If you prefer, you may call: 1-800-555-7234. Or, 202-457-2398 in metro D.C. area.

9. Please tell us about your experience with ABC employees.

ABC Sales Rep

	Excellent	Good	Unsatisfactory	No Contact
KNOWLEDGE	☐	☐	☐	☐
PROFESSIONALISM	☐	☐	☐	☐
EFFICIENCY	☐	☐	☐	☐
RESPONSIVENESS	☐	☐	☐	☐

CD-ROM Specialist

	Excellent	Good	Unsatisfactory	No Contact
KNOWLEDGE	☐	☐	☐	☐
PROFESSIONALISM	☐	☐	☐	☐
EFFICIENCY	☐	☐	☐	☐
RESPONSIVENESS	☐	☐	☐	☐

We welcome your comments and suggestions:

_____
_____
_____
_____
_____
_____
_____

All questionnaires are reviewed by C.C. Smith, Manager, Circulation Department, and ABC's CD-ROM Specialists.

RT2

August 29, 1997

Dear Customer:

Our files indicate that we recently had the opportunity to assist you with a request/concern. ABC Company, as a Global Corporation, is aware of the importance of developing and maintaining a satisfied customer base.

Please assist us by completing the enclosed questionnaire.

Sincerely,

Joe Smith
Manager
Corporate Customer Relations
ABC Company

enclosure

ABC Company Consumer Questionnaire

	Excellent	Very Good	Satisfactory	Unsatisfactory	Poor
1. THE REPRESENTATIVE'S ATTITUDE TOWARD YOU.	1 ❑	2 ❑	3 ❑	4 ❑	5 ❑
2. THE REPRESENTATIVE'S KNOWLEDGE OF YOUR CONCERN.	1 ❑	2 ❑	3 ❑	4 ❑	5 ❑
3. THE TIME FRAME IN WHICH THE REQUEST/CONCERN WAS HANDLED.	1 ❑	2 ❑	3 ❑	4 ❑	5 ❑
4. THE EASE BY WHICH THE REQUEST/CONCERN WAS HANDLED.	1 ❑	2 ❑	3 ❑	4 ❑	5 ❑
5. OVERALL, PLEASE RATE THE SERVICE PROVIDED.	1 ❑	2 ❑	3 ❑	4 ❑	5 ❑

6. WAS YOUR INQUIRY RESOLVED THROUGH THE FIRST REPRESENTATIVE YOU SPOKE WITH?

YES 1 ❑
NO 2 ❑

	Extremely	Very much	Somewhat	Not very	Not at all
7. HOW IMPORTANT TO YOUR BUYING DECISION IS OUR 24-HOUR, 7-DAY SUPPORT LINE?	1 ❑	2 ❑	3 ❑	4 ❑	5 ❑
8. HOW IMPORTANT TO YOUR BUYING DECISION IS OUR INSTANT EXCHANGE WARRANTY?	1 ❑	2 ❑	3 ❑	4 ❑	5 ❑
9. HOW IMPORTANT TO YOU IS HAVING YOUR FIRST CONTACT RESOLVE YOUR INQUIRY?	1 ❑	2 ❑	3 ❑	4 ❑	5 ❑

10. WHAT ABC PRODUCT DO YOU CURRENTLY OWN? *(check all that apply)*
    1 ❑ Printer
    2 ❑ Personal Computer
    3 ❑ Faxphone/Multipass
    4 ❑ Personal Copier
    5 ❑ Calculator
    6 ❑ Photo Camera
    7 ❑ Video Camcorder
    8 ❑ Other _____

11. WHAT PRODUCTS (ANY BRAND) ARE YOU PLANNING TO PURCHASE WITHIN THE NEXT 12 MONTHS? *(check all that apply)*
    1 ❑ Printer
    2 ❑ Personal Computer
    3 ❑ Faxphone/Multipass
    4 ❑ Personal Copier
    5 ❑ Scanner
    6 ❑ Photo Camera
    7 ❑ Video Camcorder
    8 ❑ Other _____

Any other comments: _____
_____
_____
_____

Thank you for taking the time to complete this survey. Please enclose this completed survey in the included pre-addressed, postage paid envelope.

ABC Company
123 South Lane
New York, NY 10005

Dear Customer,

Our records show that you recently required ABC Roadside Assistance service. In order to make sure that we provide the best possible service, please take a few minutes to complete the enclosed questionnaire and mail it back to us in the self-addressed, postage-paid envelope.

Thank you for your assistance.

Please circle one for each of the items:

	Excellent		Average		Poor

ROADSIDE ASSISTANCE CENTRE

Getting through to a live operator	1	2	3	4	5
Helpfulness of telephone operator	1	2	3	4	5
Handling of your request for service	1	2	3	4	5
Knowledge of operator	1	2	3	4	5
Efficiency of operator	1	2	3	4	5
Overall handling of the telephone call	1	2	3	4	5

SERVICE PROVIDED

Prompt response time by service vehicle	1	2	3	4	5
Service provided by service dealer	1	2	3	4	5
Service received was as requested	1	2	3	4	5
Appearance of the service driver's vehicle	1	2	3	4	5
Overall satisfaction with service received	1	2	3	4	5

SERVICE EXPERIENCE (Please circle one)

How long did it take for the service vehicle to arrive?

1. LESS THAN 15 MINUTES
2. 16 - 30 MINUTES
3. 31 - 45 MINUTES
4. 46 - 60 MINUTES
5. Over 60 MINUTES
6. NEVER ARRIVED

What was the main reason you called ABC Roadside Assistance? (Please circle one)

1. FLAT TIRE
2. BOOST/BATTERY PROBLEM
3. OUT OF FUEL
4. TOW
5. KEY OR LOCK PROBLEMS
6. ACCIDENT
7. STUCK
8. ENGINE PROBLEMS
9. BRAKE PROBLEMS
10. COOLING SYSTEM (FAN, RAD, ETC.)
11. ELECTRICAL PROBLEMS (EXCLUDING BATTERY)
12. TRANSMISSION PROBLEMS

OTHER (SPECIFY):_____

If your vehicle was towed, where was it towed? (Please circle one)

1. NEAREST FORD OR MERCURY DEALER
2. YOUR SELLING DEALER
3. OTHER LOCATION:_____

Do you have any suggestions or comments about ABC's Roadside Assistance services?

_____
_____
_____
_____
_____
_____
_____
_____
_____
_____
_____
_____

Thank you for completing the questionnaire.

Telephone Service
Satisfaction Questionnaire

INSTRUCTIONS

Your response to this questionnaire is completely **confidential and anonymous.** Your answers will be grouped with those of other members who have filled out other similar surveys. This information will help provide a complete and accurate picture of how well ABC serves its members, and will enable us to develop the kinds of products and services you have come to expect from ABC. **Thank you for your participation.**

---

1. Service Quality

Please check the box that indicates your personal experience with the service you received when you called the ABC Telephone Center.

YES	NO	
☐ 1	☐ 2	Employee was courteous.
☐ 1	☐ 2	Employee was easy to work with.
☐ 1	☐ 2	Employee listened to your wants and needs.
☐ 1	☐ 2	Employee asked appropriate questions to better understand your needs.
☐ 1	☐ 2	Employee made appropriate recommendations that addressed your needs.
☐ 1	☐ 2	Employee was knowledgeable about ABC policies and procedures.
☐ 1	☐ 2	Employee was knowledgeable about the product or service you called about.
☐ 1	☐ 2	All your questions were answered in easy to understand language.
☐ 1	☐ 2	The amount of time you waited to speak to an employee was acceptable.
☐ 1	☐ 2	The amount of time it took the employee to help you was acceptable.
☐ 1	☐ 2	You received the service you wanted on the first call.

When you called the Telephone Center, were you transferred to another department for further assistance?

☐ 1 YES
☐ 2 NO

Overall, how would you rate the quality of service you received on this occasion?

Excellent   **Poor**

10	9	8	7	6	5	4	3	2	1	0
☐ 10	☐ 9	☐ 8	☐ 7	☐ 6	☐ 5	☐ 4	☐ 3	☐ 2	☐ 1	☐ 0

Based on the service you received on this occasion, how likely are you to recommend ABC Federal Credit Union to an eligible friend or relative?

☐ 1 VERY LIKELY   ☐ 1 SOMEWHAT LIKELY   ☐ 1 NOT VERY LIKELY   ☐ 1 NOT AT ALL LIKELY

2. Other Information

How long have you been a member of ABC Federal Credit Union?

☐₁ LESS THAN 1 YEAR
☐₁ GREATER THAN 1 BUT LESS THAN 2 YEARS
☐₃ GREATER THAN 2 BUT LESS THAN 3 YEARS
☐₃ GREATER THAN 3 BUT LESS THAN 5 YEARS
☐₅ GREATER THAN 5 BUT LESS THAN 10 YEARS
☐₅ 10 +

Which of the following best describes your age category:

☐₁ 18 TO 24 YEARS   ☐₃ 35 TO 44 YEARS   ☐₅ 55 TO 64 YEARS
☐₂ 25 TO 34 YEARS   ☐₄ 45 TO 54 YEARS   ☐₆ 65 OR OLDER

Which of the following best describes your employment status?

☐₁ EMPLOYED FULL-TIME   ☐₃ RETIRED
☐₂ EMPLOYED PART-TIME   ☐₄ NOT EMPLOYED

Which of the following categories best describes your total household income?

☐₁ LESS THAN $25,000   ☐₄ $50,000 TO $74,999   ☐₇ $125,000 TO $149,999
☐₂ $25,000 TO $34,999   ☐₅ $75,000 TO $99,999   ☐₈ $150,000 OR MORE
☐₃ $35,000 TO $49,999   ☐₆ $100,000 TO $124,999

ABC would appreciate any additional comments or suggestions, favorable or unfavorable, that you might care to offer concerning the quality of service you received.

_____
_____
_____
_____
_____
_____
_____
_____

OPTIONAL

If you would like an ABC representative to contact you about any issues, please print your name and daytime telephone number below.

Your Name:_____   Telephone Number: (___)_____

THANK YOU FOR YOUR HELP!

Please return the questionnaire in the envelope provided to:
Market Research Services • P O Box 999 • New York, NY 10038

RT5

(Company logo)

ABC Car Inc.
Post Office Box 9999
Springfield, MA 78009
(617) 777-7777
Fax (617) 777-7788

April 8, 1998

<<First Name>> <<Last Name>>
<<Company>>
<<Address1>>
<<Address2>>
<<City>>, <<State>> <<Postal Code>>
<<Country>>

Dear <<Title>> <<LastName>>:

The Customer Service Team is responsible for handling new vehicle and optional equipment orders from the time you place an order through the time you receive your product(s). Your Customer Order Manager is your single point of contact on issues arising from the point of order submission through the time of delivery.

To help monitor the level of service we provide, we conduct regular quarterly surveys. You have been chosen to provide an assessment on the Customer Order Manager whose name appears on the enclosed questionnaire. Your honest feedback is necessary to help this person better understand his/her strengths and to realize opportunities for improvement. We greatly appreciate the time you will spend in assisting us.

This questionnaire is completely confidential and anonymous (unless you elect to provide your name). Your input will be combined with ratings of others. The Customer Order Manager will not see your individual ratings.

When you have completed the questionnaire, please mail it to us in the postage-paid envelope. Thank you for your assistance.

Sincerely,

John Smith
Director, Customer Service & Sales Administration

ABC Car Inc.
Customer Service Questionnaire

At ABC Car, it is important to us to make sure that we provide you with a quality product and quality customer service. When placing new golf car and utility vehicle orders, your primary contact is your Customer Order Manager. Would you please take a moment to complete this short questionnaire so that we can assure that we are providing the highest possible customer service to you on a regular basis? Thank you for your time.

Rating Scale

	ALWAYS	USUALLY	SOMETIMES	NEVER	NOT APPLICABLE
1. The Customer Order Manager who assisted me with my order was responsive to my needs.	4	3	2	1	0
2. My orders(s) was accurately processed and my my order(s) was delivered as agreed.	4	3	2	1	0
3. When I had a question, the Customer Order Manager answered my questions promptly.	4	3	2	1	0
4. The Customer Order Manager was knowledgeable about ABC Car products.	4	3	2	1	0
5. The Customer Order Manager gave helpful suggestions regarding the details of my order and the products ordered.	4	3	2	1	0
6. The Customer Order Manager took the time necessary to answer my questions in a satisfactory manner.	4	3	2	1	0
7. When the Customer Order Manager did not know the answer to a question, they researched the answer and responded back to me in a timely manner.	4	3	2	1	0
8. When I made a change to my order, the change was processed quickly and correctly. If the change could not be made, an alternative suggestion was provided.	4	3	2	1	0
9. The Customer Order Manager maintained a positive attitude and professionalism at all times.	4	3	2	1	0
10. The Customer Order Manager demonstrated initiative and tenacity in resolving any problems encountered.	4	3	2	1	0

Comments: _____
_____
_____

Thank you.   Your Customer Order Manager is   <<COM>>

Date:_____ Customer Name: (Optional)_____

(Company logo)

Customer Service Questionnaire

Date: _____

Account Number (optional): _____

	YES	NO
1. Was the representative courteous?	☐	☐
2. Were your questions answered satisfactorily?	☐	☐
3. Was the attitude of the staff appropriate?	☐	☐
4. Was your representative knowledgeable?	☐	☐
5. Was the service provided promptly?	☐	☐

Please return in the enclosed stamped self-addressed envelope.

FOR EMPLOYEE RECOGNITION PURPOSES ONLY

Dear Flight Attendant:

Service Provided Today By:

_____
(Name)

We are focused on providing you with friendly, timely and quality service every day. We would like to recognize our employees if we achieved these goals. Please indicate your level of satisfaction with the service we have provided.

EXCELLENT____   GOOD____   FAIR____   POOR____

F/A Name:_____ F/A #:_____ Date:_____ Flt. #_____

We welcome your comments.

_____

_____

Please return this self addressed/stamped postcard to my attention so we may properly recognize our employees and provide you with the highest level of service you have come to expect from Company ABC.

Sincerely,
Joe Smith
Director Customer Service

CALLER SATISFACTION QUESTIONNAIRE

Please rate your satisfaction with the *most recent* call you made to ABC Company for each of the following areas:

	Far Below My Expectations	*Below* My Expectations	*Met* My Expectations	*Exceeded* My Expectations
1. THE *FRIENDLINESS* OF THE REPRESENTATIVES.	1	2	3	4
2. THE *PROMPTNESS* IN WHICH YOU WERE CONNECTED TO A REPRESENTATIVE.	1	2	3	4
3. THE REPRESENTATIVE'S *KNOWLEDGE.*	1	2	3	4
4. THE *CLARITY* OF THE EXPLANATION.	1	2	3	4
5. *OVERALL SATISFACTION* WITH THE PHONE CALL.	1	2	3	4

Comments: _____

_____

_____

BUSINESS REPLY MAIL

FIRST CLASS PERMIT NO 6370 NEW YORK NY

postage will be paid by addressee

ABC COMPANY INC.
PO BOX 8898
SANTA BARBARA, CA 93103

NO POSTAGE
NECESSARY IF
MAILED IN THE
UNITED STATES

RT9

HOW ARE WE DOING?
CUSTOMER SERVICE HELP DESK CUSTOMER QUESTIONNAIRE

During the past 10 days you made a call to the Customer Service Help Desk at the ABC National Council. As part of our efforts to provide the highest level of service, we are asking a representative sample of our customers to rate the service you received on a few important areas. Since only a select few have been sent questionnaires, it is vital we receive your response. The feedback you provide will assist us in improving our services in the future. If you have questions concerning this questionnaire, call the Customer Service Help Desk at 2244 and ask for Jane Smith. Thank you for your participation.

Please indicate your level of satisfaction or dissatisfaction with the service that you received during your recent call to the Customer Service Help Desk on the following specific areas. Please circle one number on the scale for each statement.

	VERY SATISFIED			VERY DISSATISFIED

1. When placing your call to the help desk, the representative:

Took your call in a timely manner 5   4   3   2   1

Understood your question/problem....................................5   4   3   2   1

2. The representative that resolved your problem:

Resolved your problem in a timely manner 5   4   3   2   1

Handled problem in a professional manner 5   4   3   2   1

Demonstrated knowledge of equipment 5   4   3   2   1

Enter the name (if known) of the representative who resolved you problem: _____

3. Please indicate level of satisfaction with the overall
service you received. 5   4   3   2   1

4. Why did you answer question 3 the way you did? Please be specific.

_____
_____
_____
_____
_____
_____
_____
_____
_____

Please return this completed form using the enclosed return envelope.

Thank you,   INTERNAL USE ONLY:_____

Jane Smith
Manager, Customer Service Help Desk

Dear Valued ABC Paging Network Customer:

We at your local ABC office want to provide you with the best service and paging technology available. To ensure we are focusing our efforts on issues most important to our customers, please tell us your opinions using the survey below. For your convenience, we have included a postage-paid envelope.

Thank you,

If you would like an ABC representative to contact you, please check the box below

ABC Paging Network of «office»

 «name»

 «company»

 «address1»

 «address2»

 «city» «state» «zip»

Please contact me ❏

at ( ) -

Reason I would like to be contacted:

_____

_____

Your answers will remain strictly confidential unless you specify otherwise.

ABC Paging Network Inc.
Customer Satisfaction Questionnaire

1. Overall, how satisfied are you with ABC as your paging company?

	VERY SATISFIED				VERY DISSATISFIED	DON'T KNOW
	5	4	3	2	1	DK

2. How satisfied were you with these aspects of ABC's sales process:

	VERY SATISFIED				VERY DISSATISFIED	DON'T KNOW/ NO EXPERIENCE
a. The <u>telephone</u> sales representative's knowledge about ABC products/services?	5	4	3	2	1	DK/NE
b. The <u>in-person</u> sales representative's knowledge of ABC products/services?	5	4	3	2	1	DK/NE
c. The <u>in-person</u> sales representative's ability to match the pager and features to your needs?	5	4	3	2	1	DK/NE
d. Overall, how satisfied were you with ABC's <u>sales process</u>?	5	4	3	2	1	DK/NE

3. Thinking of the last time you had questions for ABC, did you <u>call</u> or <u>go into</u> the ABC office?

    1. I CALLED THE ABC OFFICE

    2. I WENT INTO THE ABC OFFICE

    3. A REPRESENTATIVE CAME TO MY HOME OR OFFICE (SKIP TO QUESTION 8)

    4. I HAVE NOT HAD TO CONTACT ABC WITH QUESTIONS (SKIP TO QUESTION 8)

4. About how long ago was this contact?

1. LESS THAN 3 MONTHS AGO	3. MORE THAN 6 MONTHS BUT LESS THAN 12 MONTHS
2. MORE THAN 3 MONTHS BUT LESS THAN 6 MONTHS	4. MORE THAN 12 MONTHS AGO

5. What was the main reason you called or went into the ABC office most recently? (*circle <u>one</u> answer*)

1. NAME/ADDRESS CHANGE	6. NOT RECEIVING PAGES CONSISTENTLY
2. UPDATE SERVICES OR PAGER	7. BROKEN PAGER
3. BILLING QUESTION	8. PRICING OR RATE INFORMATION
4. LOST PAGER	9. OTHER (*specify*) _____
5. QUESTIONS ABOUT HOW TO USE MY PAGER	

6. Thinking of this most recent experience, how satisfied were you with the following aspects of service from the *customer service rep* you worked with <u>on the phone</u> or at the <u>ABC office</u>:

	VERY SATISFIED				VERY DISSATISFIED	DON'T KNOW/ NO EXPERIENCE
a. Ability to answer questions?	5	4	3	2	1	DK/NE
b. Ability to solve problems?	5	4	3	2	1	DK/NE
c. Amount of time required to answer questions?	5	4	3	2	1	DK/NE
d. Amount of time required to solve problems?	5	4	3	2	1	DK/NE
e. Follow through on promises?	5	4	3	2	1	DK/NE
f. Overall, how satisfied were you with the ABC customer service representative on this occasion?	5	4	3	2	1	DK/NE

7. a. Was your issue resolved?   ❑ YES

                                      ❑ NO

    b. How many contacts with ABC did it take to get this issue resolved? _____# of contacts

8. Since getting your pager, has an ABC field service representative <u>come to your home or office</u> to deliver another pager or answer your questions?

   1. YES, LESS THAN 3 MONTHS AGO

   2. YES, 3 OR MORE BUT LESS THAN 6 MONTHS AGO

   3. YES, 6 OR MORE BUT LESS THAN 12 MONTHS AGO

   4. YES, MORE THAN 12 MONTHS AGO

   5. NO ABC REP HAS VISITED MY HOME OR OFFICE SINCE I SIGNED UP FOR SERVICE
      (SKIP TO QUESTION 10)

9. Thinking about your last contact with the field service representative who <u>visited your home or office</u>, how satisfied were you with the following aspects of service from this representative:

	VERY SATISFIED				VERY DISSATISFIED	DON'T KNOW/ NO EXPERIENCE
a. Speed of returning calls?	5	4	3	2	1	DK/NE
b. Ability to answer questions/solve problems?	5	4	3	2	1	DK/NE
c. Amount of time required to answer questions/solve problems?	5	4	3	2	1	DK/NE
d. Follow through on promise?	5	4	3	2	1	DK/NE
e. Keeping you updated on ABC products and services?	5	4	3	2	1	DK/NE
f. Overall, how satisfied were you with the <u>field service rep</u> who served your account on this occasion?	5	4	3	2	1	DK/NE

10. Thinking of your most recent call to ABC, how was the telephone answered?

    1. BY A PERSON/RECEPTIONIST

    2. BY AN AUTOMATED ANSWERING SYSTEM

    3. I HAVE NEVER CALLED ABC (SKIP TO QUESTION 12)

    4. DON'T RECALL HOW PHONE WAS ANSWERED (SKIP TO QUESTION 12)

11. How satisfied are you with the following aspects of how your call was answered?

	VERY SATISFIED				VERY DISSATISFIED	DON'T KNOW/ NO EXPERIENCE
a. Professionalism of the person/message?	5	4	3	2	1	DK/NE
b. Being directed to the correct person?	5	4	3	2	1	DK/NE

c. Amount of time "on hold"?	5	4	3	2	1	DK/NE
d. Overall, how satisfied are you with ABC's <u>receptionist/answering system</u>?	5	4	3	2	1	DK/NE

12. What one improvement could your local ABC office make to maximize the value you get from ABC?

_____

_____

13. Do you plan to continue using ABC during the
next six months?   1. YES   2. NO   3. DON'T KNOW

14. Would you recommend ABC to a friend or colleague?   1. YES   2. NO   3. DON'T KNOW

15. Do you have nationwide coverage with ABC?   1. YES   2. NO   3. DON'T KNOW

16. Can your pager receive <u>written</u> messages,
as well as telephone numbers?   1. YES   2. NO   3. DON'T KNOW

17. How long have you been an ABC customer? (*circle only one response*)

1. LESS THAN 3 MONTHS

2. MORE THAN 3 MONTHS BUT LESS THAN
   6 MONTHS

3. MORE THAN 6 MONTHS BUT LESS THAN 1 YEAR

4. MORE THAN 1 YEAR BUT LESS THAN
   3 YEARS

5. MORE THAN 3 YEARS BUT LESS THAN
   5 YEARS

6. MORE THAN 5 YEARS

18. May ABC follow-up with you regarding this questionnaire if they have questions? (*Your answers will remain confidential if you say "No."*)

1. YES

2. NO

THANK YOU FOR YOUR INPUT!

ABC Company
Service Center

Our records indicate that you recently contacted the ABC Service Center by phone and spoke to one of our representatives. In order to help us evaluate and improve our level of service, we are asking that you take a few moments and fill out the following Customer Questionnaire.

	VERY SATISFIED	SATISFIED	DISSATISFIED	VERY DISSATISFIED
1. Was your call answered in a timely manner?	☐	☐	☐	☐
2. Was the customer service representative you spoke with courteous?	☐	☐	☐	☐
3. Was the information provided to you clear?	☐	☐	☐	☐
4. Did you feel the information provided was accurate?	☐	☐	☐	☐
5. Were you satisfied overall with the call?	☐	☐	☐	☐

6. Are there any additional comments on how we can improve our services? _____
_____
_____

7. What additional services would you like to see in the ABC Service Center?
_____
_____

Thank you for participating in our survey. All answers are strictly confidential. Your answers will help us improve our services.

Please fold in half and staple or tape shut and return to address on the back.

If you would like, please note your name and number below

Name:_____ Phone:_____

PATIENT SATISFACTION SURVEY

Recently you were treated by the physician(s) and staff of ABC Sports Medicine Inc. Because we take pride in providing the best care to our patients, we ask that you take the time to rate our care and services. Please be candid — if we did well, your opinion will encourage our staff, but if we did not, your comments will help us improve.

Office You Visited
- ☐ Five Mill Office
- ☐ Blue Ash Office
- ☐ Eastgate Office
- ☐ Christ. Hosp. Med. Bldg.
- ☐ Western Hills Office
- ☐ Northgate Office

Doctor You Saw:
- ☐ Dr. Smith
- ☐ Dr. Feingold
- ☐ Dr. Alexandra
- ☐ Dr. Miles
- ☐ Dr. Reilly
- ☐ Dr. Jones
- ☐ Dr. Meetch
- ☐ Dr. Lee
- ☐ Dr. Sanderson
- ☐ Dr. Wilson
- ☐ Dr. Green
- ☐ Dr. Burns
- ☐ Dr. Kossel
- ☐ Dr. Plano

	Very Dissatisfied	Dissatisfied	Neutral	Satisfied	Very Satisfied
	1	2	3	4	5

When You Called...

1) The ease of getting through on the phone — 1 2 3 4 5
2) The friendliness of the phone operator — 1 2 3 4 5
3) Ease of getting an appointment at a date and time convenient for you — 1 2 3 4 5
4) The convenience of office hours — 1 2 3 4 5

When You Arrived...

5) The courtesy and helpfulness of the receptionist — 1 2 3 4 5
6) The length of time you waited before seeing the physician — 1 2 3 4 5

When you received your care...

7) The quality of service you received from our physician — 1 2 3 4 5
8) The quality of service you received from our clinical staff — 1 2 3 4 5
9) The length of time the physician spent with you — 1 2 3 4 5
10) The clarity of the physician's explanation of the required medical treatment — 1 2 3 4 5
11) The physician's responsiveness to phone calls related to your care — 1 2 3 4 5
12) The helpfulness of the staff in scheduling surgery — 1 2 3 4 5

When you were checking out or had billing questions...

13) The ease of check-out procedures — 1 2 3 4 5
14) How questions about your bill or account were answered in the office — 1 2 3 4 5
15) How questions about your bill or account were answered when calling the number on the bill — 1 2 3 4 5

16) What can we do to improve the care we provide? _____
_____
_____

17) Did anyone give you outstanding service? ☐ YES ☐ NO

If so, who was that individual and what did they do for you?
_____
_____

Patient's Name (Optional)_____ Date of Visit_____

ABC Sports Medicine Inc.
254 Old Mill Road
Cincinnati, OH 45200

Customer Satisfaction Questionnaire

In order to provide the best service to our customers, the Information Center (formerly called Help Desk) is interested in your evaluation of our computer support. Please take a few minutes to complete this survey and return it to the Information Center at _____.

Thank you!

1.   **Overall,** how satisfied are you with the support you receive from the Information Center? (PLEASE CIRCLE ONE RESPONSE.)

Very Dissatisfied								**Very Satisfied**
1	2	3	4	5	6	7	8	9

2.   Please rate the service you received from the Information Center Analyst who assisted you and the overall service you received from the Information Center. To do this, use a 1 to 9 scale, where 1 means Disagree Completely and 9 means Agree Completely. You can use 1, 9 or any number in between. (CIRCLE ONE RESPONSE FOR EACH ITEM.)

	Disagree Completely								**Agree Completely**

About the Information Center Analyst:

Was polite	1	2	3	4	5	6	7	8	9
Was knowledgeable	1	2	3	4	5	6	7	8	9
Communicated well	1	2	3	4	5	6	7	8	9
Was helpful	1	2	3	4	5	6	7	8	9
Provided accurate answers	1	2	3	4	5	6	7	8	9
Worked until the problem was solved	1	2	3	4	5	6	7	8	9
Solved problem in a reasonable time frame	1	2	3	4	5	6	7	8	9
Met my expectations	1	2	3	4	5	6	7	8	9

About the Information Center overall:

Service hours are convenient	1	2	3	4	5	6	7	8	9
Keeps me informed of progress on calls that cannot be resolved immediately	1	2	3	4	5	6	7	8	9
Meets target dates/times it gives me	1	2	3	4	5	6	7	8	9

3.   In an average week, how often do you call the Information Center? (WRITE THE NUMBER BELOW.)

_____ number of times you call the Information Center in an average week.

THANK YOU FOR YOUR HELP!

WHAT IS YOUR OPINION OF ABC CORPORATION?

To better serve you, we would like to know your opinion of the quality of our service at ABC Corporation. You recently have received, or are receiving, service from our company. Please indicate the extent to which you agree or disagree with the following statements about the service you received from the staff. We've included a pre-paid envelope for the return of your comments. Thank you in advance for helping us better service the needs of our customers.

	Low				High
1. The salespeople:					
a) understand my business	1	2	3	4	5
b) offer services appropriate to my needs	1	2	3	4	5
c) respond promptly to my requests	1	2	3	4	5
2. The staff is knowledgeable about the services they offer	1	2	3	4	5
3. My Account Team is:					
a) accessible	1	2	3	4	5
b) responsive to my needs	1	2	3	4	5
4. My Account Team:					
a) advises me promptly of any problems	1	2	3	4	5
b) readily offers me solutions to any problem that may occur	1	2	3	4	5
5. ABC Corp. staff have a professional attitude in their dealings with me.	1	2	3	4	5
6. ABC Corp. delivers what they promise the right way and on time.	1	2	3	4	5
7. My invoices from ABC Corp. are:					
a) accurate	1	2	3	4	5
b) timely	1	2	3	4	5
8. ABC Corp. keeps up with the latest in technologies to better service my needs.	1	2	3	4	5
9. I would recommend ABC Corp. to other companies.	1	2	3	4	5

The best way that ABC Corp. could further its service to my company is:

_____

_____

_____

Your additional thoughts or comments: _____

_____

Thank you for taking the time to complete this questionnaire. Your views and comments will help us improve our service to you.

Chapter 3

Product/Process Improvement Questionnaires

Although recent transaction questionnaires have value, there will be circumstances when firms will want to concentrate on soliciting feedback directly related to improving their products and/or processes. The product/process improvement questionnaire is more effective for this purpose.

Purpose

To understand your customers' satisfaction with existing products/processes and solicit suggestions for improvement.

Characteristics

- Greater presence of open-ended questions. As discussed in Chapter 1, it is this style of question that is conducive to obtaining ideas as opposed to limiting your customer to the response sets provided.

- Future-oriented rather than past-oriented. This characteristic is inherent in the fact that these questionnaires focus on suggestions rather than evaluations.

- Feedback is explicit. Whereas the decisions to improve products or processes as a result of feedback from a recent transaction questionnaire is derived from the responses, feedback in these questionnaires is explicit. Customers are specifically asked how the firms products/processes can be improved.

Pitfalls

- The increased use of open-ended questions makes this type of questionnaire more expensive to process. This is due to the increased time needed to sort the responses prior to tabulating the results.

- The presence of open-ended questions will also impact the response rate as customers are more likely to experience fatigue due to the additional effort required to answer this style of questionnaire and thus fail to complete the questionnaire. This will result in either a lower response rate or in incomplete questionnaires being returned.

- In order for your customers to provide you with useful suggestions for improvement, their experiences with your firm must be memorable. This requires that the experience be either recent, reoccurring or significant. Otherwise, the detail provided in their open-ended questions may be insufficient to take action.

Benefits

✓ Feedback is not transaction or time dependent.

Unlike recent transaction questionnaires, product/process improvement questionnaires are not limited to actual transactions with your company, nor is time necessarily a factor in the reliability of the responses. Feedback from these questionnaires is usually based on many experiences that may have occurred over a long period of time.

✓ Opportunity to obtain ideas that can truly lead to "top box" customer satisfaction.

When it comes to obtaining ideas from your customers, their collective experiences represent a wealth of information that, if mined effectively, can provide you with the information to delight your customer. With this in mind, it is important that firms not get caught in the trap of throwing money toward value-added services at the expense of what customers believe to be essential services. The argument, as put forth by Noriaki Kano, which became known as the Kano Model, is quite compelling.

The KANO Model (the "Model") represents the correlation between your customer's level of fulfillment and their level of satisfaction with respect to specific product or process elements such as time of delivery, reliability of product or service, or the knowledge level of company representatives.

Each of these product or process elements, from your customer's perspective, fall within one of the following groups:

Attractive Quality

Elements: The elements that provide satisfaction when fulfilled but do not lead to dissatisfaction when not fulfilled.

Example: Your customer orders a product from you to be delivered on a specific day. They indicate that they are in a rush to receive it. You manage to get the order to them earlier than promised and charge them for a normal delivery.

One-Dimensional Quality

Elements: The elements that result in satisfaction when fulfilled and result in dissatisfaction when not fulfilled.

Example: Your customer orders a product to be delivered on a specific day. If it is delivered on time, your customer is satisfied. If it is delivered late, your customer is dissatisfied.

Must-Be Quality

Elements: The elements which are taken for granted when fulfilled but result in dissatisfaction and defection when not fulfilled.

Example: Your customer orders a product from you to be delivered on a specific day. When the truck arrives, the driver gets out of his truck and brings the product to your front door. The fact that the product was delivered to your door as opposed to you taking it out of the truck yourself is taken for granted. However, had the driver expected you to take it from the truck, you would likely be dissatisfied and may defect to a competitor.

Each of these three elements are drawn on a graph below to illustrate their implications on both customer satisfaction and fulfillment.

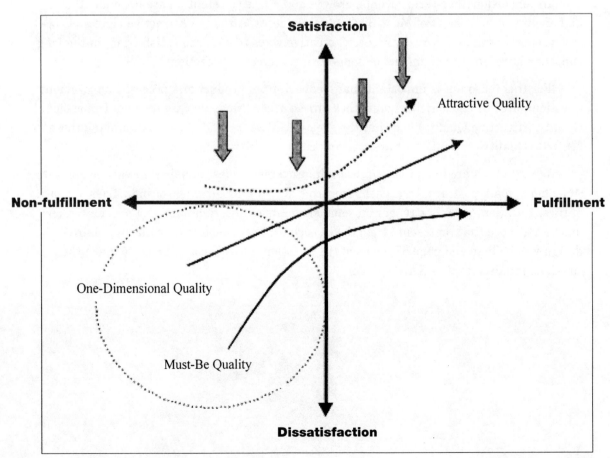

With reference to the graph on page 55, your focus should be on the Must-Be Quality and One-Dimensional Quality elements in the quadrant indicated by the circle. This quadrant represents the elements that require the greatest improvement.

Attractive Quality elements which are located in the upper right quadrant pertain primarily to marketing, promotional and service attributes that a company uses to attract new customers, further satisfy existing customers and further differentiate themselves from their competitors. Attractive Quality elements are inherently unstable and face tremendous downward pressure from both the increased expectations of the customer and reactions by competitors.

To illustrate, consider the experience of going to a movie theatre. New theatres with comfortable and spacious seating, large screens, THX Dolby® Digital sound systems and unique food options can be classified as Attractive Quality elements. There is no doubt that these elements increase customer satisfaction and fulfillment, however, as more movie theatres are constructed with the same Attractive Quality elements, the downward pressure of increased customer expectations will eventually transform these elements from Attractive Quality to Must-Be Quality elements. It is within these Must-Be Quality elements that most service breakdowns occur. It is therefore within this element that attention must be paid.

In conclusion, long-term revenue growth and effective retention are dependent on a high degree of fulfillment of Must-Be Quality elements. Although Attractive elements represent short-term, and in many respects, creative ways to enhance satisfaction, in the long run, they have little or no impact on long-term customer satisfaction.

For this reason, it is important that feedback from product and process improvement questionnaires be categorized among these three areas (Must-Be Quality, One-Dimensional Quality, Attractive Quality) and that the greatest effort be made toward improving those Must-Be Quality elements that are creating customer dissatisfaction.

What follows are five product/process improvement questionnaires in various formats (telephone, mail, postcard, Internet) from firms across a broad range of industries. As each of these questionnaires is stronger on some elements of questionnaire design and weaker on others, those that represent strengths in each of the six elements of questionnaire design will be listed on page 57. None of the questionnaires is constructed to make the distinctions required for the KANO Model.

Questionnaire Design Elements	Questionnaire Numbers				
	1	2	3	4	5
Questionnaire Layout		✓			
Questionnaire Content	✓	✓	✓	✓	✓
Questionnaire Flow	✓	✓	✓	✓	✓
Questionnaire Structure	✓	✓			✓
Questionnaire Wording	✓	✓	✓		✓
Questionnaire Reliability**	✓	✓	✓	✓	

** The ability to assess the validity of a questionnaire is highly dependent on knowing the objective of each survey project. As the objectives specific to your organization will likely be unique, any questionnaires that appear in this box will be based on issues of reliability only.

Customer Survey

Customer Name: _____

Product(s) Purchased _____   Date: _____

PURCHASE EXPERIENCE;

Are you a: (*Please check the appropriate box*)   Did you: (*Check each that applies*)
1. ☐ First-time user   1. ☐ Visit the dealership
2. ☐ Existing user   2. ☐ Representative visited you
                                                     3. ☐ Both

Why did you choose ABC equipment? (*Check each that applies*)
1. ☐ Price   7. ☐ Reputation/Referral
2. ☐ Quality   8. ☐ Product Features
3. ☐ Previous Use   9. ☐ Dealer Suggested
4. ☐ System Compatibility   10.☐ Don't Know
5. ☐ Service/Warranty   11.☐ Other - Specify _____
6. ☐ Product/Appearance   _____

How did you choose the dealership? (*Check each that applies*)
1. ☐ Location   5. ☐ Previous Purchase Experience
2. ☐ Referral   6. ☐ Deal Services Products
3. ☐ Advertising   7. ☐ Don't Know
4. ☐ Yellow Pages   8. ☐ Other - Specify _____
                                      _____

USING A SCALE FROM 1 TO 5 RATE THE FOLLOWING ATTRIBUTES

5 = VERY SATISFIED ◄──► 1 = VERY DISSATISFIED

	5	4	3	2	1
The accessibility of our dealership:	☐	☐	☐	☐	☐
The ease of doing business with our dealership:	☐	☐	☐	☐	☐
Our prices:	☐	☐	☐	☐	☐
The professionalism of our salesperson:	☐	☐	☐	☐	☐
Our salesperson's knowledge of communication equipment:	☐	☐	☐	☐	☐
Our salesperson's understanding of your needs:	☐	☐	☐	☐	☐
Overall Satisfaction Buying from our Dealership:	☐	☐	☐	☐	☐

FROM A DELIVERY STANDPOINT, HOW SATISFIED ARE YOU WITH:

	5	4	3	2	1
Delivery of the product on time:	☐	☐	☐	☐	☐
Completeness of delivery:	☐	☐	☐	☐	☐
Overall Satisfaction with Delivery:	☐	☐	☐	☐	☐

PI1

RATE THE FOLLOWING ATTRIBUTES USING THIS SCALE

VERY SATISFIED ◄──► *VERY DISSATISFIED*

FROM AN EQUIPMENT PERSPECTIVE, HOW SATISFIED ARE YOU WITH:

	5	4	3	2	1
The ease of using the equipment:	☐	☐	☐	☐	☐
The audio quality:	☐	☐	☐	☐	☐
The product durability:	☐	☐	☐	☐	☐
Battery life (if applicable):	☐	☐	☐	☐	☐
Communication range or distance:	☐	☐	☐	☐	☐
Competitiveness of product price:	☐	☐	☐	☐	☐
Product being water resistant:	☐	☐	☐	☐	☐
Warranty and dealer services:	☐	☐	☐	☐	☐
Overall Satisfaction with the Product:	☐	☐	☐	☐	☐

FROM A TRAINING STANDPOINT, HOW SATISFIED ARE YOU WITH;

	5	4	3	2	1
The training on how to use the product:	☐	☐	☐	☐	☐
Having your questions answered in an easy to understand manner:	☐	☐	☐	☐	☐
The explanation of warranty and services:	☐	☐	☐	☐	☐
Overall Satisfaction with Training:	☐	☐	☐	☐	☐

USING A SCALE FROM 1 TO 5 ANSWER THE FOLLOWING QUESTIONS

VERY LIKELY ◄──► *VERY UNLIKELY*

	5	4	3	2	1
How likely are you to recommend our dealership to others?	☐	☐	☐	☐	☐
How likely are you to recommend this product to others?	☐	☐	☐	☐	☐
How likely are you to repurchase from our dealership?	☐	☐	☐	☐	☐
How likely are you to purchase additional products in the future?	☐	☐	☐	☐	☐

Comments, please provide comments that will help us serve you better in the future:

_____

_____

_____

_____

Would you like a follow-up call from our management team?   Yes ☐   No ☐

ABC Bank

Please check the box beside **the ABC Bank branch that you deal with most often.**
If this branch is not included in the list below, write in the name and location of the
branch you deal with most often. *(Please indicate **one** branch only.)*

	To assist in processing your answers, please fill in boxes as follows:
	☑ or ☒ or ■

Ⓐ YOUR OVERALL SATISFACTION

I. How satisfied are you overall with the service at this branch? **Please rate on the 10-point scale where 1 = Extremely Dissatisfied and 10 = Extremely Satisfied.**

Extremely Dissatisfied									Extremely Satisfied
1	2	3	4	5	6	7	8	9	10
☐	☐	☐	☐	☐	☐	☐	☐	☐	☐

II. If you were to take out a new financial product or service with any financial institution in the next six months, how likely would you be to get it from this branch?

Definitely would not get it	Probably would not get it	Might or might not get it	Probably would get it	Definitely would get it
☐	☐	☐	☐	☐

III. How likely would you be to recommend this branch to a friend or business associate?

Definitely would not recommend	Probably would not recommend	Might or might not recommend	Probably would recommend	Definitely would recommend
☐	☐	☐	☐	☐

IV. If it were possible to switch all of your ABC Bank business to another financial institution with no hassle, how likely is it that you would stay with ABC Bank?

Definitely would not stay	Probably would not stay	Might or might not stay	Probably would stay	Definitely would stay
☐	☐	☐	☐	☐

V. Taking into consideration your own experience as well as anything you may have read, seen or heard, how would you rate the overall quality of **the branch you deal with** most often?

Poor	Fair	Good	Very Good	Excellent
☐	☐	☐	☐	☐

VI. Taking into consideration your own experience with financial institutions, as well as anything you may have read, seen or heard, how would you rate the overall quality of **ABC Bank as a financial institution?**

Poor	Fair	Good	Very Good	Excellent
☐	☐	☐	☐	☐

VII. When you consider the various types of fees you pay for ABC Bank's services in relation to what other banks charge for similar services, would you say that ABC Bank is....

Very high priced	High priced	About the same	Low priced	Very low priced
☐	☐	☐	☐	☐

VIII. Considering ABC Bank's overall quality in relation to the cost of its products and services, would you say that ABC Bank offers...

Poor value for the money	Fair value	Good value	Very good value	Excellent value for the money
☐	☐	☐	☐	☐

Ⓑ YOUR SATISFACTION WITH THE WAY WE SERVE YOU

These questions are based on your most recent experiences (within the last 6 months) with the ABC Bank branch you deal with most often. Please rate how you feel about this branch's performance for each attribute on a 10-point scale where 1=Extremely Dissatisfied and 10=Extremely Satisfied. If the attribute does not apply to you, please check N/A.

	Extremely Dissatisfied								Extremely Satisfied		N/A
	1	2	3	4	5	6	7	8	9	10	
Staff make me feel my business is appreciated	☐	☐	☐	☐	☐	☐	☐	☐	☐	☐	☐
I can trust the staff I deal with	☐	☐	☐	☐	☐	☐	☐	☐	☐	☐	☐
Staff have authority to resolve problems	☐	☐	☐	☐	☐	☐	☐	☐	☐	☐	☐
Staff give me straightforward answers	☐	☐	☐	☐	☐	☐	☐	☐	☐	☐	☐
Staff reassure me that my problems will be solved	☐	☐	☐	☐	☐	☐	☐	☐	☐	☐	☐
Staff help me realize/achieve my long term financial goals	☐	☐	☐	☐	☐	☐	☐	☐	☐	☐	☐
Staff deal with me tactfully and with understanding when I apply for a loan, mortgage or credit card	☐	☐	☐	☐	☐	☐	☐	☐	☐	☐	☐
The application process for a loan, mortgage or credit card is simple	☐	☐	☐	☐	☐	☐	☐	☐	☐	☐	☐
Interest rates are competitive	☐	☐	☐	☐	☐	☐	☐	☐	☐	☐	☐
Hours of business are convenient	☐	☐	☐	☐	☐	☐	☐	☐	☐	☐	☐

Ⓒ PROBLEMS WITH YOUR BRANCH

Listed below are some problems that research tells us customers sometimes experience with their bank. Please check the box for all those you experienced in the past 6 months, with the ABC Bank branch you deal with most often.

I have had no problems with my branch in the past 6 months ☐ ➔ **PLEASE GO TO D.**

Day-to-day dealings with this branch

1. Staff lacked knowledge of ABC Bank products and services ☐
2. Staff unable to recommend the best way of meeting my needs ☐
3. Staff did not do what I asked ☐
4. Staff not responsive to my requests ☐
5. Staff did not do what they said they would do ☐
6. Staff did not return my phone call ☐
7. Branch manager was not available when I needed to see him or her ☐
8. Staff attitude was not positive ☐
9. Staff is rude, unfriendly or inconsiderate ☐
10. Transaction not handled quickly and efficiently ☐
11. Bank policy not clearly explained ☐

Continued top right ⎯⎤

Loans, mortgages and credit cards

➔ 12. Slow response to my application for a loan, mortgage or credit card ☐
13. No reasonable explanation given when turned down for a loan, mortgage or credit card ☐

Cashing and chequing policies

14. Returned cheque or missed payment not handled with tact and courtesy ☐
15. Cheque cashing not easy ☐

Problem solving

16. Staff did not contact me promptly when mistake occurred ☐
17. Staff did not correct mistake quickly ☐

D   AUTOMATED BANKING MACHINES (ABMs)

Listed below are some problems that research tells us customers sometimes experience with ABMs. Please check the box for all those you experienced while dealing with your branch's ABM in the past 6 months.

Do you use the ABM at your branch?   yes ☐ **Continue**

no ☐ ➤ **PLEASE GO TO E.**

Have you had any problems with your branch's ABM in the past 6 months?   yes ☐ **Continue**

no ☐ ➤ **PLEASE GO TO E.**

Problems with your branch's ABM.

18. ABM did not work   ☐

19. Location of ABM not safe   ☐

20. ABM would not give me enough cash because of a hold on my deposit   ☐

21. ABM does not offer all the banking services I'd like   ☐

E   YOUR MOST SERIOUS PROBLEM

IF YOU HAD NO PROBLEMS WITH EITHER THE BRANCH (C) OR ITS ABM (D), PLEASE GO TO F.

If you did have a problem, please continue with this question.

I.   For all the problems you have just checked in (C) and (D), which one would you consider the most serious?   ☐☐ (Write number from 01 to 21)

II.   Did you tell anyone at ABC Bank about it?   yes ☐   no ☐ ➤ **PLEASE GO TO F.**

III.   Overall, how satisfied were you with ABC Bank response to the problem? (Check one only)

Completely satisfied	Not completely satisfied, but the action taken was acceptable	Not completely satisfied, but some action was taken	Not at all satisfied with the action taken	Not at all satisfied because no action was taken
☐	☐	☐	☐	☐

F   A LITTLE ABOUT YOU

In order to help classify some of the information we collect, we would like you to answer a few additional questions. Please check the appropriate box in each question.

I.   Is ABC Bank your main financial institution?

yes ☐

no ☐

II.   Which best describes your total annual household income, before taxes?

Up to $30,000	☐	$75,001 – $100,000	☐
$30,001 – $45,000	☐	$100,001 – $150,000	☐
$45,001 – $75,000	☐	Over $150,000	☐

III.   Which age group are you?

Under 18	☐	45 – 54	☐
18 – 24	☐	55 – 64	☐
25 – 34	☐	65 and over	☐
35 – 44	☐		

IV.   Are you?

Male ☐   Female ☐

Ⓖ FINAL THOUGHTS

Is there anything else you would like to tell us?

*If you have a **specific problem** to which you'd like a response, please bring it to the attention of your Branch Manager. If you have already raised this with the Branch Manager and you are not satisfied, please contact the appropriate Vice-President whose name and phone number are listed in the binder at your Branch's INFORMATION CENTRE.*

Ⓗ MAY WE SHARE?

If you would like to be identified, please print your name and address.

Name: _____   Telephone: _____

Address: _____

_____   Date: _____

Thank you very much for your time.
It will make a difference.

Please return your completed questionnaire in the enclosed postage-paid envelope to:

ABC Bank

ABC Engineering Laboratories, Inc.

Digital Protective Relaying Seminar
Montreal, Quebec, Canada
May 1998

Thank you for providing us with information we will use to better serve your present and future protection needs.

Name _____ Title _____
Company _____
Address _____
City, State, Zip _____
E-Mail _____ Phone _____ Fax _____

What information did you find most valuable? _____
_____
_____

What information did you find least valuable? _____
_____
_____

Are you currently buying equipment?
    Yes
    No

    If yes, in what category?
    ___Automation   ___Transmission   ___Subtransmission
    ___Communications   ___Distribution   ___Other, please specify

What product or service would you like to see ABC enhance? _____
_____
_____

Do you require additional information about a specific product or service? _____
_____
_____

May we contact you? _____

Making Electric Power Safer, More Reliable, and More Economical

Corporate Customer Service
Customer Questionnaire

Your response to the following Customer Service activities/responsibilities will give us an insight as to how we are performing compared to other Hospital Customer Service companies. Please circle the appropriate number or letter. We would appreciate your honest and specific comments if 1, 2, or U are circled.

	POOR	BELOW AVERAGE	AVERAGE	GOOD	OUTSTANDING	COMPARED TO OTHER HEALTHCARE COMPANIES		COMMENTS
						FAVORABLE	UNFAVORABLE	
1. Courtesy displayed by ABC Customer Service Personnel	1	2	3	4	5	F	U	
2. Ease of using Customer Service 1-800 ABC Phone #	1	2	3	4	5	F	U	
3. Speed of answering phones	1	2	3	4	5	F	U	
4. Speed/accuracy in taking your order	1	2	3	4	5	F	U	
5. Responsiveness to your question								
a. Backorder Status	1	2	3	4	5	F	U	
b. Returned Goods	1	2	3	4	5	F	U	
c. Shipping Dates	1	2	3	4	5	F	U	
d. Rush Orders/Emergency Orders	1	2	3	4	5	F	U	
e. Assistance for Product Alternatives	1	2	3	4	5	F	U	
f. Overall Product knowledge	1	2	3	4	5	F	U	
g. Timeliness of return response if question can't be answered on first phone call	1	2	3	4	5	F	U	
h. Status of your order	1	2	3	4	5	F	U	
i. Handling of credits in a timely manner	1	2	3	4	5	F	U	
6. ABC's Performance of "on time delivery" of your orders	1	2	3	4	5	F	U	
7. Demonstration of a proactive approach to your customer service needs								
8. The overall quality of ABC's responsiveness to your your customer service needs	1	2	3	4	5	F	U	

Corporate Customer Service
Customer Questionnaire
(cont'd)

This next section is for your comments relative to the preceding ratings. We welcome your suggestions and comments and would appreciate your candid remarks — positive or negative. When referring to specific questions, please put the number next to your comment, i.e., 5.a. Let us know where we fall short compared to other Health Care Companies.

#

_____

_____

9. Is our competition offering additional services ABC should also consider?

COMPETITION   WHAT COMPETITION OFFERS:
(Name of Company)

_____   _____

_____   _____

10. What other Customer Service areas should we examine for future improvement? Please be specific.

_____

_____

_____

11. Do you currently order electronically from ABC?   ☐ YES
                                                           ☐ NO

If no would you be interested?   ☐ YES
                                                           ☐ NO

Who should we contact?   Name _____

                              Address _____

                              Phone #: (___) _____

Return survey to:
ABC Company
Corporate Customer Service
500 Lexington Lane
Chicago, IL 60611

ABC Company E-Mail Response Questionnaire

We would appreciate your candid appraisal of ABC's e-mail service and will use your feedback to help us to continue improving our service to you. Your feedback is extremely valuable to us and we appreciate your time spent answering our questions. All responses will be kept confidential. Please feel free to use the questionnaire to address any concerns, issues or ideas that you might have specific to communicating with ABC through e-mail. If you have any questions regarding the questionnaire, you may e-mail us at network@abc.com.

To get started click on "reply," type your response to complete the questionnaire, and when you are finished please e-mail it back to us at ****. If you have any questions regarding the questionnaire, you may e-mail us at ****.

Note: For your ease in viewing the questionnaire, maximize your e-mail screen if possible.

The questionnaire contains 12 questions (nine multiple choice and three questions for your open comments and suggestions) and should take about six minutes to complete. Thank you again for your assistance in completing this questionnaire.

(1) Please rank each of the following in order of importance by using number 1 to indicate most important *(using each number 1 through 4 just once).*

[ ] Formality and professionalism of ABC's response
[ ] Response short and concise, not too lengthy
[ ] Speed of the delivery of our response
[ ] Anticipating your future needs in addition to answering your question

(2) How would you prefer we respond to your e-mail? *(Please put an X next to all that apply.)*
[ ] Through e-mail
[ ] With a phone call
[ ] Allow you to indicate in each e-mail whether you want an e-mail or phone call

Please refer to the details of the e-mail(s) you sent to answer the next 10 questions. *(Indicate your answer by typing an X next to how you would rate the response received from E-Mail Response.)*

(3) How would you rate the timeliness of the response(s) sent to you?
[ ] Excellent
[ ] Very good
[ ] Good
[ ] Fair
[ ] Poor
[ ] Not applicable

(4) How would you rate the information and assistance given to you by the E-Mail Response representative?
[ ] Excellent
[ ] Very good
[ ] Good
[ ] Fair
[ ] Poor
[ ] Not applicable

(5) Please rate the response you received in terms of being clear, being complete and answering all your question(s)?
[ ] Excellent
[ ] Very good
[ ] Good

[ ] Fair
[ ] Poor
[ ] Not applicable

(6) How would you rate your overall satisfaction with ABC E-Mail Response?
[ ] Excellent
[ ] Very good
[ ] Good
[ ] Fair
[ ] Poor
[ ] Not applicable

(7) Did E-Mail Response provide information that was helpful to your investment decision process?
[ ] Excellent
[ ] Very good
[ ] Good
[ ] Fair
[ ] Poor
[ ] Not applicable

The next two questions relate to your overall impression of our e-mail service and how it helps you communicate with ABC. The answers to these questions will help us determine how effective our e-mail site is as a communication channel compared to our other channels of communication. Please indicate your answer by typing an X next to how you would rate the response received from the E-Mail Response team.

(8) Based on your previous e-mail interaction(s), how likely are you to use e-mail again to communicate with ABC?
[ ] Extremely likely
[ ] Somewhat likely
[ ] Neutral
[ ] Somewhat unlikely
[ ] Extremely unlikely

(9) What are your thoughts of receiving e-mail updates on new or enhanced ABC products and services?
[ ] Extremely valuable
[ ] Somewhat valuable
[ ] Neutral
[ ] Not interested
[ ] Do not send these to me

We sincerely value your opinions. The questions below are designed to allow you to openly communicate your comments and ideas. Please indicate your thoughts about the following:

(10) What ABC e-mail features and enhancements would you like to see to better meet your needs?

(11) What e-mail features and benefits do other companies offer that you find beneficial?

(12) Please describe any other specific comments or suggestions that may help us improve our level of e-mail service?

Once again, thank you for your assistance in completing this questionnaire.

ABC Company

Chapter 4

Overall Customer Satisfaction Questionnaires

Purpose

To obtain an understanding of your customer's satisfaction across a broad range of areas.

Characteristics

- Measures satisfaction in a broad range of areas, some of which customers may not have been exposed to in their transactions with the company.

Unlike recent transaction or process/product improvement questionnaires that are typically tied to specific experiences with a company, overall satisfaction questionnaires are often so broad that most of your customers will not have sufficient breadth of experience with your company to provide answers based on actual experiences with every attribute. In these cases, answers will be based on perception rather than on experience. Because negative word of mouth erodes customer loyalty, one may argue that perception and experience are one and the same. Although true for customer loyalty, when it comes to prioritizing the attributes on which to take action, the feedback that is most reliable is that provided by a customer's actual experience as the feedback tends to more accurately reflect a company's performance.

- Multiple-Transaction vs. Single-Transaction Oriented.

During the interviews we conducted with providers of overall satisfaction questionnaires, we found that the purpose of the questionnaires was to gauge customer satisfaction based on the fact that their customers have had multiple interactions with their companies.* Using the questionnaire in this manner requires that the customer have interacted with your company for a minimum period of time prior to being surveyed.** To do otherwise would create inconsistencies in the reporting of the information as you may be measuring the satisfaction of your customers of 10 years along with those who had been with you for as little as three months. This would clearly form a bias as those who had only been with you for a short period of time would not have had the opportunity to form as grounded an opinion as those who had been dealing with your company longer. This is particularly true in the case of expensive goods where people often give higher ratings to rationalize their purchasing decision. (Refer to Halo Effect, page 29, for an expanded discussion of this issue.) In the cases where sufficient time has passed to negate the bias of the Halo Effect, it is wise to identify the length of time your customer has been dealing with your company in the demographics sections of your questionnaire. This will allow you to compare and contrast attribute ratings based on length of time with the company to better understand how this characteristic impacts the results of your study.

* The minimum time required will vary depending on the industry and product or services involved.

** This characteristic also applies to product/process improvement questionnaires.

Pitfalls

• Questionnaires tend to be too long and/or complex.

When constructing this type of questionnaire, there is a temptation to ask far more questions than are really necessary for the objectives of your study. In Chapter 1, we discussed the importance of defining your objective when embarking on a survey project in order to keep the questionnaire focused. It is understandable that companies will want to measure all possible opportunities for their customers to form an impression of their company (moments of truth) and there is certainly value in doing so. However, excessively long questionnaires (greater than eight pages) and/or questionnaires with complex skip patterns are necessary but will end up frustrating your customers.

Benefits

✓ Opportunity to recreate a presence with your customer.

Provides an opportunity to remind your customers of your presence and generate sales.

✓ Value as a tracking mechanism of attributes identified in your recent transaction and product/process improvement questionnaires.

Problem areas uncovered in your recent transaction and process improvement questionnaires can be measured in your overall satisfaction questionnaire. Doing so will enable you to track your effectiveness in resolving these problems.

✓ Appropriate data-gathering tool where high frequency of transactions doesn't lend itself to transaction-based measurement.

Your customers may engage in so many transactions that to ask your customers to complete a questionnaire for each transactional experience is unrealistic and will ultimately irritate them. The overall satisfaction questionnaire, which is not transaction-dependent, yet encompasses aspects of your business, would be an effective way to survey these customers.

What follows are 12 overall satisfaction questionnaires in various formats (telephone, mail, postcard, Internet) from firms across a broad range of industries. As each of these questionnaires is stronger on some elements of questionnaire design and weaker on others, those that represent strengths in each of the six elements of questionnaire design will be listed below.

Questionnaire Design Elements	Questionnaire Numbers											
	1	2	3	4	5	6	7	8	9	10	11	12
Questionnaire Layout	✓	✓		✓	✓	✓				✓		
Questionnaire Content	✓	✓	✓	✓	✓	✓		✓			✓	✓
Questionnaire Flow	✓	✓		✓		✓	✓	✓	✓	✓	✓	✓
Questionnaire Structure	✓	✓		✓	✓	✓	✓				✓	✓
Questionnaire Wording	✓	✓	✓	✓	✓	✓	✓		✓			✓
Questionnaire Reliability**	✓	✓	✓	✓	✓	✓		✓	✓	✓		

** The ability to assess the validity of a questionnaire is highly dependent on knowing the objectives of each survey project. As the objectives specific to your organization will likely be unique, any questionnaires that appear in this box will be based on issues of reliability only.

ABC Co. Customer Satisfaction Questionnaire

Please mark survey in the following manner:

Use blue or black pen, or pencil. Completely fill the response choice as shown in the example:

Correct Mark: ○ ● ○ ○

Other types of marks cannot be recognized when the form is scanned by a computer. Thank you for your attention to these details.

1. Select the one **category** that **most closely describes** your organization:

   ☐ BIOTECHNOLOGY   ☐ GENERAL MANUFACTURER
   ☐ CHEMICAL MANUFACTURER   ☐ INDEPENDENT TESTING LAB
   ☐ ENVIRONMENTAL   ☐ PHARMACEUTICAL
   ☐ CONSUMER PRODUCTS   ☐ SEMICONDUCTORS

2. Please choose the **one** category that **most closely describes** *your* job function:

   ☐ QUALITY CONTROL   ☐ RESEARCH SCIENTIST
   ☐ LAB TECHNICIAN   ☐ PURCHASING
   ☐ STOCKROOM   ☐ CHEMIST
   ☐ WAREHOUSE   ☐ ENGINEER
   ☐ PRODUCTION   ☐ SAFETY/ENVIRONMENTAL/
   ☐ QUALITY ASSURANCE   REGULATORY
          ☐ OTHER: _____

3. What is your responsibility regarding the purchase of chemicals?

   ☐ MAKE DECISION ON WHICH BRAND TO BUY
   ☐ RECOMMEND BRAND TO BUY
   ☐ SPECIFY REQUIREMENTS
   ☐ NONE

4. Please rate your overall level of satisfaction with ABC Co.

   ☐ VERY SATISFIED
   ☐ SATISFIED
   ☐ NEITHER SATISFIED NOR DISSATISFIED
   ☐ DISSATISFIED
   ☐ VERY DISSATISFIED

5. How would you rate ABC Co. among the chemical brands you buy:

   ☐ THE BEST
   ☐ AMONG THE BEST
   ☐ ABOUT THE SAME
   ☐ AMONG THE WORST
   ☐ THE WORST

6. Please read carefully the following list of attributes. Then rank each attribute (First through Fifth) in order of importance to you, with FIRST CHOICE being the **MOST** important and FIFTH CHOICE being the **LEAST** important. Mark only one circle per choice.

   A. Product Availability   D. Customer Service
   B. Product Quality   E. Technical Service
   C. Value for the Price

	Attribute (mark one per choice)				
First Choice	A	B	C	D	E
Second Choice	A	B	C	D	E
Third Choice	A	B	C	D	E
Fourth Choice	A	B	C	D	E
Fifth Choice	A	B	C	D	E

7. Please tell us what we can do to increase your level of satisfaction with ABC products and services.

   _____
   _____
   _____
   _____
   _____

8. The following is a list of statements concerning ABC products. Please read the statements carefully and mark the response that most closely represents your experience with ABC chemicals.

	STRONGLY AGREE	AGREE	NEITHER AGREE NOR DISAGREE	DISAGREE	STRONGLY DISAGREE
Overall, I am satisfied with the **quality** of ABC chemicals	☐	☐	☐	☐	☐
Product specification match my requirements	☐	☐	☐	☐	☐
I am satisfied with the quality of packages supplies by ABC	☐	☐	☐	☐	☐
ABC offers the variety of chemicals I need	☐	☐	☐	☐	☐
ABC products perform as expected	☐	☐	☐	☐	☐
I can get the product in the package sizes I need	☐	☐	☐	☐	☐
ABC packages are easy to open and close	☐	☐	☐	☐	☐
Labels on the product are easy to read	☐	☐	☐	☐	☐
The packages protect the product from contamination	☐	☐	☐	☐	☐
The packages protect users from harm	☐	☐	☐	☐	☐
Overall, I am satisfied with the value I receive from ABC chemicals	☐	☐	☐	☐	☐
ABC chemicals provide good value for the price	☐	☐	☐	☐	☐
ABC chemicals are fairly priced.	☐	☐	☐	☐	☐

I have used the ABC Internet site	☐ YES	☐ NO
The Internet site is useful to me	☐ YES	☐ NO

How do you purchase ABC chemicals? ☐ DIRECT FROM ABC CO. ☐ THROUGH A DISTRIBUTOR

	STRONGLY AGREE	AGREE	NEITHER AGREE NOR DISAGREE	DISAGREE	STRONGLY DISAGREE
Overall, I am satisfied with the **availability** of ABC chemicals	☐	☐	☐	☐	☐
I receive the quantity I order	☐	☐	☐	☐	☐
I receive the products I order	☐	☐	☐	☐	☐
The products I order arrive on time	☐	☐	☐	☐	☐
The products I order arrive in good condition	☐	☐	☐	☐	☐
The packing list contains the information I need	☐	☐	☐	☐	☐
Overall, I am satisfied with the **technical service** provided by ABC	☐	☐	☐	☐	☐
The Technical Service Representative answers my questions in one call	☐	☐	☐	☐	☐
I can reach a Technical Service Representative on the first try	☐	☐	☐	☐	☐
The Technical Service Representative provides the information I need	☐	☐	☐	☐	☐
Product complaints are resolved promptly	☐	☐	☐	☐	☐
Product complaints are resolved to my satisfaction	☐	☐	☐	☐	☐
Overall, I am satisfied with the **customer service** provided by my supplier	☐	☐	☐	☐	☐
I can reach my Customer Service Representative on the first try	☐	☐	☐	☐	☐
My Customer Service Representative answers my questions in one call	☐	☐	☐	☐	☐
My Customer Service Representative provides the information I need	☐	☐	☐	☐	☐
Service problems are resolved promptly	☐	☐	☐	☐	☐
Service problems are resolved to my satisfaction	☐	☐	☐	☐	☐
It is easy to obtain Certificates of Analysis	☐	☐	☐	☐	☐
It is easy to obtain Material Safety Data Sheets	☐	☐	☐	☐	☐

I use the ABC catalog to order chemicals	☐ YES	☐ NO
I use the distributor's catalog to order chemicals	☐ YES	☐ NO

☐ Mark here if you would like a copy of the ABC Co. 1998/99 catalog.

Name _____ Title _____

Company _____ Department _____

Street Address _____ Telephone _____

ABC ORIENTAL RUGS

In order to improve and maintain the highest standard of customer service in the industry, we are constantly monitoring our staff and looking for new ways to improve! Please take a moment to answer these quick questions.
Thank you very much in advance for completing this quick questionnaire!

A. How would you rate:	Excellent	Very Good	Good	Average	Poor
(1) your overall experience at ABC Oriental Rugs?	O	O	O	O	O
(2) your salesperson's knowledge of rugs?	O	O	O	O	O
(3) the attentiveness of your salesperson?	O	O	O	O	O
(4) the promptness of our delivery service?	O	O	O	O	O
(5) the politeness of our sales staff?	O	O	O	O	O
(6) our overall selection?	O	O	O	O	O

	YES	DON'T KNOW	NO
B. Would you return to ABC Oriental Rugs in the future?	O	O	O
C. Would you refer others to ABC Oriental Rugs?	O	O	O
D. Did you find the rug you were looking for?	O	O	O

E. Did you purchase a rug? What affected your decision?
_____
_____

If you answered Don't Know or No, please indicate why:
_____
_____

Your Additional Comments Are Appreciated:
_____
_____

ABC PLASTICS CORPORATION USA
Customer Questionnaire

COMPANY
CUSTOMER STREET ADDRESS
CUSTOMER CITY, STATE ZIP CODE

Product(s) Purchased: Territory:

If any of the above name or address information is incorrect or out-of-date, we apologize for the inconvenience and kindly request your assistance to make any necessary corrections so that we may update our records. Thank you!

Please circle the response which you feel most accurately describes how satisfied you are with ABC Plastics Corporation's performance in the **last 12 months**. If you are not familiar with a specific area of ABC Plastics Corporation's service, please skip to the next question. Your assistance is very much appreciated.

CUSTOMER SERVICE

	VERY SATISFIED	SOMEWHAT SATISFIED	SOMEWHAT DISSATISFIED	VERY DISSATISFIED	DON'T KNOW/ NOT APPLICABLE
How do you rate the following:					
1. Speed of our Customer Service Representative (CSR) in answering your call?	4	3	2	1	DK/NA
2. Willingness of CSR to help?	4	3	2	1	DK/NA
3. Effectiveness of CSR in processing orders?	4	3	2	1	DK/NA
4. Effectiveness of CSR in resolving problems?	4	3	2	1	DK/NA
5. Accuracy of information provided by CSR?	4	3	2	1	DK/NA

Comments: _____
_____

MARKETING & SALES

	VERY SATISFIED	SOMEWHAT SATISFIED	SOMEWHAT DISSATISFIED	VERY DISSATISFIED	DON'T KNOW/ NOT APPLICABLE
1. Are you satisfied with the frequency of visits you receive from your Sales Representative?	4	3	2	1	DK/NA
2. How do you rate the timeliness of Marketing/Sales response to your pricing and information requests?	4	3	2	1	DK/NA
3. How do you rate your Marketing/Sales Rep's understanding of your needs?	4	3	2	1	DK/NA

	VERY SATISFIED	SOMEWHAT SATISFIED	SOMEWHAT DISSATISFIED	VERY DISSATISFIED	DON'T KNOW/ NOT APPLICABLE
4. How do you rate the Pricing of our products?	4	3	2	1	DK/NA

TECHNICAL SUPPORT

	VERY SATISFIED	SOMEWHAT SATISFIED	SOMEWHAT DISSATISFIED	VERY DISSATISFIED	DON'T KNOW/ NOT APPLICABLE
1. How do you rate the level of knowledge of our Technical Support Team?	4	3	2	1	DK/NA
2. How do you rate our ability to resolve production problems in an effective manner?	4	3	2	1	DK/NA
3. How do you rate our ability to solve problems in a timely manner?	4	3	2	1	DK/NA
4. How satisfied are you with the documentation (Certificate of Analysis) provided by our Technical Department?	4	3	2	1	DK/NA

Comments: _____

_____

TRAFFIC/SHIPPING

	VERY SATISFIED	SOMEWHAT SATISFIED	SOMEWHAT DISSATISFIED	VERY DISSATISFIED	DON'T KNOW/ NOT APPLICABLE
1. How do you rate our ability to ship your orders on time?	4	3	2	1	DK/NA
2. How do you rate the transit time for delivery of your orders?	4	3	2	1	DK/NA
3. How do you rate our response to your emergency delivery requests?	4	3	2	1	DK/NA
4. Do you receive your shipping documentation (Bill of Lading, Shipping Notice) in a timely manner?	4	3	2	1	DK/NA
5. How do you rate the accuracy of information provided by our Traffic Department?	4	3	2	1	DK/NA
6. How do you rate the timely response to requests made to our Traffic Department?	4	3	2	1	DK/NA

OS3

Please indicate the type of shipments you receive:

Bulk Tracks ○

Bulk Railcars ○

Gaylord Boxes ○

25kg Bags ○

Super Sacks ○

Other ○

Comments: _____

_____

PRODUCTS

	VERY SATISFIED	SOMEWHAT SATISFIED	SOMEWHAT DISSATISFIED	VERY DISSATISFIED	DON'T KNOW/ NOT APPLICABLE
1. Is ABC Plastics Company meeting your specifications for incoming raw materials?	4	3	2	1	DK/NA
2. How do you rate the packaging of our products?	4	3	2	1	DK/NA
3. What are your most important criteria for product quality? _____					
4. How would you rate ABC Plastics Corporation versus these criteria?	4	3	2	1	DK/NA

Comments: _____

_____

OVERALL

	VERY SATISFIED	SOMEWHAT SATISFIED	SOMEWHAT DISSATISFIED	VERY DISSATISFIED	DON'T KNOW/ NOT APPLICABLE
1. Overall, how satisfied are you with ABC Plastics Corp., U.S.A.?	4	3	2	1	DK/NA
2. How satisfied are you with the ease of doing business with ABC?	4	3	2	1	DK/NA
3. How satisfied are you with using our toll free number (888/ABC-USA3)?	4	3	2	1	DK/NA

4. Would you recommend to your organization that it continue to use ABC Plastics Corporation as a supplier?

DEFINITELY WOULD RECOMMEND	PROBABLY WOULD RECOMMEND	PROBABLY WOULD NOT RECOMMEND	DEFINITELY WOULD NOT RECOMMEND
4	3	2	1

5. Considering ABC Plastics' performance in the last 12 months, is ABC Plastics' performance:
_____ Better _____ About the Same _____ Worse

If our rating above is not categorized as "Better" would you kindly provide your recommendations as to how we can improve this rating to meet your satisfaction?

_____

_____

6. Please list what you consider to be the three most important areas of performance when dealing with a raw material supplier.

_____

_____

_____

7. Are there any other comments you would like to make regarding ABC Plastics Corporation's performance?

_____

_____

Thank you for your assistance. The information you share with us will help us to better serve your needs.

Name of person completing this questionnaire (optional) _____

Please print the name of your ABC Marketing and Sales Representative (optional) _____
Comments: _____

_____

OS4

Contact Name: _____   Emp. # _____

Contact Address: _____   Dist/Br # _____

_____

_____

Telephone Number: _____

I'm calling from the office of ABC's Vice President of Customer Service.

Our goal at ABC Company is to provide you with the kind of service that meets your needs and exceeds your expectations. It is important to us that all of our customers receive prompt, efficient, courteous and professional service. To help us see how we are doing in these areas, if you would please spare a couple of moments to answer a few questions. The answer choices are: Very Satisfied, Satisfied, Dissatisfied and Very Dissatisfied. Please rate the following:

	Very Satisfied	Satisfied	Dissatisfied	Very Dissatisfied
ABILITY TO REACH CUSTOMER SERVICE	O	O	O	O
RESPONSE TIME MET YOUR EXPECTATIONS	O	O	O	O
SERVICE REPRESENTATIVE WAS FRIENDLY...............................	O	O	O	O
SERVICE REPRESENTATIVE SHOWED SINCERE INTEREST IN RESOLVING YOUR PROBLEMS.............................	O	O	O	O
SERVICE REPRESENTATIVE KEPT YOU INFORMED ON STATUS OF YOUR EQUIPMENT	O	O	O	O
SERVICE REPRESENTATIVE HAD THE KNOWLEDGE TO ANSWER YOUR QUESTIONS	O	O	O	O
REPAIRS WERE PERFORMED AT THE TIME PROMISED	O	O	O	O
REPAIRS WERE COMPLETED IN A TIMELY MANNER	O	O	O	O
EQUIPMENT REPAIRED TO YOUR SATISFACTION..........................	O	O	O	O
QUALITY OF THE WORK PERFORMED	O	O	O	O
OVERALL SERVICE RATING	O	O	O	O

Product Repaired:

_____

Date Call Opened:

_____

Incident #:

What could we do to better serve you?

_____

_____

_____

Comments:

_____

_____

Name of person completing the questionnaire (optional): _____

Service Representative (if known): _____

Would you like to be contacted concerning: New Product Information   ◯ Yes
          ◯ No

                                   Service Maintenance Programs   ◯ Yes
          ◯ No

Joe Smith, our Senior Vice President, sincerely appreciates your time and assistance.

ABC Company Customer Questionnaire

Please Check One:

I   Customer Service

1. How would you rate the overall of quality of our customer service performance?

☐ Completely Dissatisfied   ☐ Dissatisfied   ☐ Neither Satisfied nor Dissatisfied   ☐ Satisfied   ☐ Completely Satisfied

2. How would you rate the customer service representative assigned to servicing your account?

☐ Completely Dissatisfied   ☐ Dissatisfied   ☐ Neither Satisfied nor Dissatisfied   ☐ Satisfied   ☐ Completely Satisfied

3. How would you rate the ability of the customer service representative to answer your questions?

☐ Completely Dissatisfied   ☐ Dissatisfied   ☐ Neither Satisfied nor Dissatisfied   ☐ Satisfied   ☐ Completely Satisfied

4. How would you rate our overall customer service in comparison to our competitor's performance?

☐ Completely Dissatisfied   ☐ Dissatisfied   ☐ Neither Satisfied nor Dissatisfied   ☐ Satisfied   ☐ Completely Satisfied

5. If you could make one change or suggestion in this area, what would it be?

_____

_____

II   Customer Order and Shipping

1. How would you rate our order fill?

☐ Completely Dissatisfied   ☐ Dissatisfied   ☐ Neither Satisfied nor Dissatisfied   ☐ Satisfied   ☐ Completely Satisfied

2. How would you rate our turnaround time as measured from time we receive your order to the time you receive it?

☐ Completely Dissatisfied   ☐ Dissatisfied   ☐ Neither Satisfied nor Dissatisfied   ☐ Satisfied   ☐ Completely Satisfied

3. How would you rate the condition of your shipment?

☐ Completely Dissatisfied   ☐ Dissatisfied   ☐ Neither Satisfied nor Dissatisfied   ☐ Satisfied   ☐ Completely Satisfied

4. How would you rate the accuracy of the shipment you received?

☐ Completely Dissatisfied   ☐ Dissatisfied   ☐ Neither Satisfied nor Dissatisfied   ☐ Satisfied   ☐ Completely Satisfied

5. How would you rate the shipping documents and packing list as to providing the information you need to process your shipment?

☐ Completely Dissatisfied   ☐ Dissatisfied   ☐ Neither Satisfied nor Dissatisfied   ☐ Satisfied   ☐ Completely Satisfied

6. How would you rate our VOR program?

☐ Completely Dissatisfied   ☐ Dissatisfied   ☐ Neither Satisfied nor Dissatisfied   ☐ Satisfied   ☐ Completely Satisfied

7. How would you rate us in the above categories as compared to our competitors?

☐ Completely Dissatisfied   ☐ Dissatisfied   ☐ Neither Satisfied nor Dissatisfied   ☐ Satisfied   ☐ Completely Satisfied

8. If you could make one change or suggestion in this area, what would it be?

_____

_____

III   Customer Returns/Claims

1. How would rate us in processing core returns?

☐ Completely Dissatisfied   ☐ Dissatisfied   ☐ Neither Satisfied nor Dissatisfied   ☐ Satisfied   ☐ Completely Satisfied

2. How would you rate our response time for processing warranty?

☐ Completely Dissatisfied ☐ Dissatisfied ☐ Neither Satisfied nor Dissatisfied ☐ Satisfied ☐ Completely Satisfied

3. How would you rate us in processing stock returns?

☐ Completely Dissatisfied ☐ Dissatisfied ☐ Neither Satisfied nor Dissatisfied ☐ Satisfied ☐ Completely Satisfied

4. How would you rate us in issuing you a credit for the above?

☐ Completely Dissatisfied ☐ Dissatisfied ☐ Neither Satisfied nor Dissatisfied ☐ Satisfied ☐ Completely Satisfied

5. How would you rate us in the above categories as compared to our competitors?

☐ Completely Dissatisfied ☐ Dissatisfied ☐ Neither Satisfied nor Dissatisfied ☐ Satisfied ☐ Completely Satisfied

6. If you could make one change or suggestion in this area, what would it be?

_____

_____

IV Technical Support

1. How would you rate our responses to resolving your technical inquires?

☐ Completely Dissatisfied ☐ Dissatisfied ☐ Neither Satisfied nor Dissatisfied ☐ Satisfied ☐ Completely Satisfied

2. How would you rate our response time in replying to your inquiries?

☐ Completely Dissatisfied ☐ Dissatisfied ☐ Neither Satisfied nor Dissatisfied ☐ Satisfied ☐ Completely Satisfied

3. How would you rate us in the above categories as compared to our competitors?

☐ Completely Dissatisfied ☐ Dissatisfied ☐ Neither Satisfied nor Dissatisfied ☐ Satisfied ☐ Completely Satisfied

4. If you could make one change or suggestion in this area, what would it be?

_____

_____

V Marketing Support

1. How would you rate our catalogs?

☐ Completely Dissatisfied ☐ Dissatisfied ☐ Neither Satisfied nor Dissatisfied ☐ Satisfied ☐ Completely Satisfied

2. How would you rate our trade and consumer sales literatures?

☐ Completely Dissatisfied ☐ Dissatisfied ☐ Neither Satisfied nor Dissatisfied ☐ Satisfied ☐ Completely Satisfied

3. How would you rate the attractiveness of our Major Marketing Events sales promotions?

☐ Completely Dissatisfied ☐ Dissatisfied ☐ Neither Satisfied nor Dissatisfied ☐ Satisfied ☐ Completely Satisfied

4. How would you rate the attractiveness of our Special Profit Opportunities sales promotions?

☐ Completely Dissatisfied ☐ Dissatisfied ☐ Neither Satisfied nor Dissatisfied ☐ Satisfied ☐ Completely Satisfied

5. How would you rate the effectiveness of our advertising?

☐ Completely Dissatisfied ☐ Dissatisfied ☐ Neither Satisfied nor Dissatisfied ☐ Satisfied ☐ Completely Satisfied

6. How would you rate the field sales representative assigned to service your account?

☐ Completely Dissatisfied ☐ Dissatisfied ☐ Neither Satisfied nor Dissatisfied ☐ Satisfied ☐ Completely Satisfied

7. If you could make one change or suggestion in this area, what would it be?

_____

_____

VI Product

1. How would you rate the overall quality of our products?

☐ Completely Dissatisfied ☐ Dissatisfied ☐ Neither Satisfied nor Dissatisfied ☐ Satisfied ☐ Completely Satisfied

2. How would you rate the overall packaging of our products?

☐ Completely Dissatisfied ☐ Dissatisfied ☐ Neither Satisfied nor Dissatisfied ☐ Satisfied ☐ Completely Satisfied

3. How would you rate us in the above categories as compared to our competitors?

☐ Completely Dissatisfied ☐ Dissatisfied ☐ Neither Satisfied nor Dissatisfied ☐ Satisfied ☐ Completely Satisfied

4. If you could make one change or suggestion in this area, what would it be?

_____

_____

VII Summary

In general, how would you rate doing business with us as compared to other suppliers you deal with?

☐ Completely Dissatisfied ☐ Dissatisfied ☐ Neither Satisfied nor Dissatisfied ☐ Satisfied ☐ Completely Satisfied

Optional

Company Name:_____

Respondent Name: _____Date: _____

RADIOLOGY DEPARTMENT: PATIENT QUESTIONNAIRE

Dear Valued Patient,

We would appreciate your input and request that you take just a few moments before leaving the department to complete this questionnaire. Your participation in doing this will help us to better the quality of the services that we provide.

Please check the Service(s) where you had the procedure(s) done and write the date and time of appointment:

Mammography	○	CT (Cat Scan)	○
Densitometry	○	Nuclear Medicine	○
X-Ray	○	Ultrasound	

Appointment: <u>Year/Month/Day</u>   ___:___   AM   PM
                   (Date)   *(Time)*   *(Circle One)*

Please circle your rating for the following:

	Poor	Fair	Good	Very Good	Excellent
1. Ease of getting a convenient appointment.	1	2	3	4	5
2. Processing through Outpatient Registration.	1	2	3	4	5
3. Helpfulness of our Reception Staff.	1	2	3	4	5
4. Finding your way to our department.	1	2	3	4	5
5. Finding your way around our department.	1	2	3	4	5
6. Waiting time prior to procedure(s).	1	2	3	4	5
7. Technologist's or Nurse's explanations.	1	2	3	4	5
8. Technologist's or Nurse's care & concern.	1	2	3	4	5
9. Radiologist's (physician specialist) care.	1	2	3	4	5
10. Courtesy and professionalism of our Staff.	1	2	3	4	5
11. Overall cleanliness of the Radiology Department.	1	2	3	4	5
12. The overall quality of service rendered.	1	2	3	4	5

Your comments would also be welcome (please continue on the reverse side).

_____

_____

If you would like us to follow-up with you, please provide your name, address and phone #.

_____

Please insert the completed survey into one of the white wall mounted boxes located in our waiting and exit areas, or mail to ABC Medical Center, Department of Radiology, One Springfield Center, Springfield, MA, 22000. Attn: Jane Smith, Radiology.

THANK YOU VERY MUCH! WE VALUE YOUR TIME AND INPUT! HAVE A NICE DAY...

ABC Insurance Company
Corporate Research Customer Satisfaction Questionnaire

Health Version

Hello, may I speak to Mr./Ms._____? (If not home, do not leave a message)

IF "WHO'S CALLING": My name is (TSR Name) and I am calling on behalf of ABC Insurance Company. We are conducting a brief survey. Is Mr./Ms._____ available?

IF "NOT AVAILABLE": Have a pleasant (day/evening).

IF "AVAILABLE" go to INTRODUCTION

IF "SPOUSE": I am sorry Mr./Ms._____. I am only authorized to speak with Mr./Ms._____. Thank you for your time and have a pleasant (day/evening).

INTRODUCTION:
Mr./Ms._____ my name is _____ from ABC Insurance Co. You are one of our customers and we would like to ask you about our service. All of your responses will be kept confidential, and we are not selling anything (today/this evening). It should take about 10 minutes to complete the survey, may I begin asking you some questions now?

If YES: Go to Question 1

If NO: I do want to thank you for being a policyowner with our Company. Have a good (day/evening). Good-bye.

ABC Insurance Company
Corporate Research Customer Satisfaction Questionnaire

Health Agency Version

Q1. On a scale of 1 to 6 with 1 being 'very dissatisfied,' 2 'dissatisfied,' 3 'somewhat dissatisfied,' 4 'somewhat satisfied,' 5 'satisfied' and 6 'very satisfied,' how satisfied are you: (7 Don't Know)

(Write number below)

A. OVERALL WITH ABC INSURANCE CO. _____
B. OVERALL WITH YOUR ABC HEALTH INSURANCE POLICY _____

Q2. On a scale of 1 to 6 with 1 being 'very dissatisfied,' 2 'dissatisfied,' 3 'somewhat dissatisfied,' 4 'somewhat satisfied,' 5 'satisfied' and 6 'very satisfied,' how satisfied are you with: (7 Don't Know)

(Write number below)

A. THE ACCURACY WITH WHICH ABC CO. ISSUED YOUR POLICY _____
B. THE SPEED WITH WHICH ABC CO. ISSUED YOUR POLICY _____
C. THE VALUE OF THE POLICY FOR THE MONEY YOU PAY _____

Q3. Have you ever recommended ABC Insurance Co. to a friend or relative?

A. YES **(IF YES, SKIP TO Q 11)**   B. NO

Q4. How likely are you to recommend ABC Insurance Co. to a friend or relative?

A. VERY LIKELY   B. LIKELY   C. UNLIKELY   D. VERY UNLIKELY   E. DON'T KNOW

Q5. How likely would you be to buy again from ABC Insurance Co.? *(If respondent says can't afford, re-ask question and include at start "If you could afford...")*

A. VERY LIKELY   B. LIKELY   C. UNLIKELY   D. VERY UNLIKELY   E. DON'T KNOW

Q6. Have you ever called ABC Insurance Co. using our toll free Home Office 800 number?

A. YES   B. NO **(IF NO, SKIP TO Q14)**   C. *(Do Not Read)* DON'T' KNOW **(SKIP TO Q14)**

Q7. On a scale of 1 to 6, with 1 being 'very dissatisfied,' 2 'dissatisfied,' 3 'somewhat dissatisfied,' 4 'somewhat satisfied,' 5 'satisfied' and 6 'very satisfied,' how satisfied were you with: (7 Don't Know)

(Write number below)

A. THE OVERALL SERVICE YOU RECEIVED OVER THE PHONE _____
B. THE TIME IT TOOK TO REPLY TO YOUR PHONE REQUEST _____
C. THE ACCURACY OF INFORMATION GIVEN OVER PHONE _____
D. THE FRIENDLINESS OF SERVICE YOU RECEIVED OVER THE PHONE _____
E. HAVING ANY COMPLAINTS OR PROBLEMS RESOLVED
   (IF APPLICABLE) OVER THE PHONE. _____

Q8. Have you ever filed a claim again your insurance policy?

(If YES, ask if they handled the claim or if their Hospital, Physician or a relative handled the claim.)

A. YES — (I handled the claim)
B. YES — (My Hospital, Physician or a relative handled my claim) **(SKIP TO Q16)**
C. NO — **(IF NO, SKIP TO Q16)**
D. *(Do Not Read)* DON'T KNOW **(SKIP TO Q16)**

Q9. The following set of questions deal with claim service you received from the home Office and not from your Agent or local sales office. On a scale of 1 to 6, with 1 being 'very dissatisfied,' 2 'dissatisfied,' 3 'somewhat dissatisfied,' 4 'somewhat satisfied,' 5 'satisfied' and 6 'very satisfied,' how satisfied were you with: (7 Don't Know)

(Write number below)

A. THE OVERALL CLAIM SERVICE YOU RECEIVED   _____
B. OUR ABILITY TO ANSWER YOUR CLAIMS QUESTIONS   _____
C. OUR ABILITY TO PROCESS YOUR CLAIM WITHIN A REASONABLE
   AMOUNT OF TIME   _____
D. THE COURTESY OF THE PEOPLE YOU WORKED WITH DURING THE
   CLAIMS PROCESS   _____

Q10. On a scale of 1 to 6, with 1 being 'very dissatisfied,' 2 'dissatisfied,' 3 'somewhat dissatisfied,' 4 'somewhat satisfied,' 5 'satisfied' and 6 'very satisfied,' please indicate how satisfied you are with: (7 Don't Know)

(Write number below)

A. THE OVERALL SERVICE YOU RECEIVE FROM YOUR AGENT   _____
B. THE PERSONALIZED SERVICE YOU RECEIVE FROM YOUR AGENT   _____
C. YOUR AGENT'S ABILITY TO ANSWER YOUR QUESTIONS THOROUGHLY   _____
D. YOUR AGENT'S ABILITY TO IDENTIFY YOUR INSURANCE NEEDS   _____
E. BEING ABLE TO CONTACT YOUR AGENT OR DIVISION OFFICE
   (SALES OFFICE)   _____

Q11. What is your most preferred method of communication with ABC Mutual? (only 1 answer)

A. AN AGENT   D. INTERNET
B. HOME OFFICE 800#   E. (*Do Not Read*) OTHER_____
C. MAIL

Q12. How likely is it that your financial situation will change in the next two years? Would you say it is:

A. LIKELY TO IMPROVE   C. LIKELY TO GET WORSE
B. LIKELY TO STAY THE SAME   D. (*Do Not Read*) DON'T KNOW

DEMOGRAPHICS

Now, I would like to ask a few questions about yourself.

(Write number below)

Qd1. How many children under 18 are living with you in your household?   _____

Qd2. What is your marital status? (*Read list until check*)

A. MARRIED   C. SINGLE FORMERLY MARRIED
B. SINGLE NEVER MARRIED   D. (*Do Not Read*) REFUSED

Qd3. Which of the following best describes your formal education? (*Read list until check*)

A. SOME HIGH SCHOOL (OR NONE)   D. COLLEGE GRADUATE OR GREATER
B. HIGH SCHOOL GRADUATE   E. (*Do Not Read*) REFUSED

C. SOME COLLEGE OR VOCATION TRAINING

Qd4. What is your current employment status? (*Read list until check*)

A. EMPLOYED FULL-TIME   D. RETIRED
B. EMPLOYED PART-TIME   E. NOT WORKING
C. RECEIVING DISABILITY PAYMENTS   F. (*Do Not Read*) REFUSED

(DO NOT READ) (*If both C and D, check age. If under 65 check C, if 65 or over check D*)

Qd5. Which of the following groups best represents your total annual family income before taxes? (*Read list until check*)

A. LESS THAN $15,000   E. $50,000-100,000
B. $15,000-30,000   F. $100,000 OR MORE
C. $30,000-40,000   G. (*Do Not Read*) REFUSED
D. $40,000-50,000

Qd6. How long ago did you buy your first insurance policy with ABC Mutual?

A. LESS THAN 1 YEAR   C. 5 TO 10 YEARS   E. DON'T KNOW
B. 1 TO 5 YEARS   D. MORE THAN 10 YEARS

That completes the questionnaire. Thank you for your time and participation.

Please fill out these fields after a complete questionnaire.

Policy Number: _____ Rep: _____ Today's Date: __/__/__

ABC Company

Date
Name
Title
Company
Address
Address

RE: Graphical HEC 1 Technical Support with ABC Co. member ****

Dear Name,

Thank you for using **** software. I hope your project is going well since my last contact with you. In order to maintain a high level of service, **** needs feedback from you regarding your experience with our software and support staff. We would appreciate it if you could take a few minutes to answer the following questions. Please fax or mail us your response.

(Please circle one)

Overall satisfaction with **** Technical Support	Poor	1	2	3	4	5	Excellent
Promptness of your call or email being answered	Poor	1	2	3	4	5	Excellent
Courteousness of our Technical Support personnel	Poor	1	2	3	4	5	Excellent
Knowledge of our Technical Support personnel	Poor	1	2	3	4	5	Excellent
Satisfaction with our voice mail/receptionist and the direction of your call	Poor	1	2	3	4	5	Excellent
Satisfaction with **** software you received support on	Poor	1	2	3	4	5	Excellent

Please include comments that will help us to improve our service.

_____

_____

_____

Please check one:
❏ For **** use only
❏ All or a portion of my comments may be used for marketing purposes.

Thank you again for your time, and we look forward to hearing from you.

Sincerely,
Name
Title

ABC COMPANY CUSTOMER SATISFACTION QUESTIONNAIRE

ABC is conducting this Customer Satisfaction Questionnaire in order to get an objective view of how well ABC currently meets your needs. Your most candid feedback is greatly appreciated. Please return this completed survey by fax to Jane Smith at 000-000-0000.

Please circle one rating for each of the following questions.

How do you rate the overall service you receive from us?

(Poor) 1   2   3   4   5   6 (Excellent)

Comments:

How do you rate our overall systems capabilities?

(Poor) 1   2   3   4   5   6 (Excellent)

Comments:

How do you rate our overall computer capabilities?

(Poor) 1   2   3   4   5   6 (Excellent)

Comments:

How do you rate the overall quality of our sales representatives?

(Poor) 1   2   3   4   5   6 (Excellent)

Comments:

How do you rate the overall quality of our account managers?

(Poor) 1   2   3   4   5   6 (Excellent)

Comments:

How do you rate the overall quality of our client service representatives?

(Poor) 1   2   3   4   5   6 (Excellent)

Comments:

OS9

How do you rate the consistency of our service?

(Poor) 1   2   3   4   5   6 (Excellent)

Comments:

Generally speaking, does ABC

(Check One)

exceed your expectations	❑
satisfy your expectations	❑
not live up to your expectations	❑

Comments:

What are your recommendations for improving the quality of product/service we offer you?

Given your business and industry, how do we need to change in order to continue to be your partner five years from now?

NAME AND COMPANY (optional):

ABC Logistics   (COMPANY LOGO)

HOW WELL ARE WE MEETING YOUR EXPECTATIONS?

CONSIDERING YOUR EXPERIENCE OVERALL...

Mark one response to each question.

1. How SATISFIED have you been with the services provided by **Logistics Operations** during the past 12 months?

Very Satisfied   5 ☐   4 ☐   3 ☐   2 ☐   1 ☐   Very Satisfied

If for any reason you rated **Logistics Operations** "1," "2," or "3" please explain why.

---

2. Given the choice, would you RECOMMEND **Logistics Operations** as a services supplier?

Definitely Recommended ☐10 ☐9 ☐8 ☐7 ☐6 ☐5 ☐4 ☐3 ☐2 ☐1 Definitely Not Recommended

If for any reasons you rated **Logistics Operations** a "6" or below, please explain why.

---

3. Overall, how would you rate the VALUE of the service you receive from **Logistics Operations**?

Excellent ☐10 ☐9 ☐8 ☐7 ☐6 ☐5 ☐4 ☐3 ☐2 ☐1 Bad

If for any reason you rated **Logistics Operations** a "6" or below, please explain why.

---

4. Does **Logistics Operations** FOLLOW-UP with you to ensure resolution of issues you have brought to their attention?

Always ☐10 ☐9 ☐8 ☐7 ☐6 ☐5 ☐4 ☐3 ☐2 ☐1 Never

If for any reason you rated **Logistics Operations** a "6" or below, please explain why.

---

5. Overall, how do you rate the QUALITY of the relationship you have with **Logistics Operations**?

Excellent ☐10 ☐9 ☐8 ☐7 ☐6 ☐5 ☐4 ☐3 ☐2 ☐1 Bad

If for any reason you rated **Logistics Operations** a "6" or below, please explain why.

ABC Logistics   (COMPANY LOGO)

PERFORMANCE EVALUATION

This section asks you to evaluate the performance of **Logistics Operations**. For each area below, mark a **response that best describes your opinion of Logistics Operations' performance**. If you have no experience with a particular area, mark NO OPINION. Please be candid in your evaluations. Share your comments with us at the end of the questionnaire, or attach explanatory material.

How do you rate...

	No Opinion	Excellent									Bad
1. PERSONNEL											
• Availability	☐	☐10	☐9	☐8	☐7	☐6	☐5	☐4	☐3	☐2	☐1
• Professionalism	☐	☐10	☐9	☐8	☐7	☐6	☐5	☐4	☐3	☐2	☐1
• Competence	☐	☐10	☐9	☐8	☐7	☐6	☐5	☐4	☐3	☐2	☐1
• Responsiveness	☐	☐10	☐9	☐8	☐7	☐6	☐5	☐4	☐3	☐2	☐1
• Effectiveness	☐	☐10	☐9	☐8	☐7	☐6	☐5	☐4	☐3	☐2	☐1

If for any reason you rated **Logistics Operations** a "6" or below, please explain why.

	No Opinion	Excellent									Bad
2. PRODUCT DELIVERY											
• Freight Movement	☐	☐10	☐9	☐8	☐7	☐6	☐5	☐4	☐3	☐2	☐1
• Outbound Freight Movement	☐	☐10	☐9	☐8	☐7	☐6	☐5	☐4	☐3	☐2	☐1
• Timeliness	☐	☐10	☐9	☐8	☐7	☐6	☐5	☐4	☐3	☐2	☐1

If for any reason you rated **Logistics Operations** a "6" or below, please explain why.

	No Opinion	Excellent									Bad
3. OTHER											
• NAFTA prime Activities	☐	☐10	☐9	☐8	☐7	☐6	☐5	☐4	☐3	☐2	☐1
• MAQUILA Permit Coordination	☐	☐10	☐9	☐8	☐7	☐6	☐5	☐4	☐3	☐2	☐1

If for any reason you rated **Logistics Operations** a "6" or below, please explain why.

OS10

ABC Logistics   (COMPANY LOGO)

GENERAL QUESTIONS

1. Have you had any PLEASANT or UNPLEASANT SURPRISES with **Logistics Operations** in the past 12 months? Has something happened or have you discovered something — even something small — that was better or worse than you expected? If so, please tell us about it.

PLEASANT SURPRISES(S): _____
_____
_____

UNPLEASANT SURPRISE(S): _____
_____
_____

What one area could **Logistics Operations** improve to better meet your expectations?
In what way? _____
_____
_____

3. Would you like someone to follow up with you regarding any concerns you may have? ☐ Yes ☐ No
If "**Yes**", please tell us about them and the best way to contact you. _____
_____
_____

4. Did this questionnaire provide an adequate opportunity to express your opinions about **Logistics Operations** and its services? ☐ Yes ☐ No   If "**NO**," why not?_____
_____
_____

5. What Line of Business are you associated with?

☐ PCN   ☐ Broadband

☐ EN   ☐ CSO

☐ EN DATA   ☐ Other _____

☐ Wireless

6. Which of the following best describes your primary job function? **Mark only one response.**

☐ Engineering   ☐ Maintenance   ☐ Purchasing

☐ Executive Mgmt.   ☐ Marketing   ☐ Sales

☐ Finance   ☐ Operations   ☐ Other (specify) _____

☐ I/S   ☐ Planning   _____

THANK YOU FOR TAKING THE TIME
TO COMPLETE THIS QUESTIONNAIRE

OS11

ABC
Healthcare

ABC Medical Service Center   Delivering Excellence

To improve our service to you, we need to know how we are doing. Please take the time to fill out this survey on your assigned ABC Medical Service Center Customer Service Representative,_____.
If you would prefer to discuss your service with the Supervisor of this employee, please contact
_____ at 1-800-333-8111 at extension _____.

	Excellent	Very good	On average	Fair	Need improvements	Not applicable
RESPONSIVENESS (Timely and appropriate responses)						
Answering phone calls	5	4	3	2	1	N/A
Replying to correspondence (e.g. faxes, letters, etc.)	5	4	3	2	1	N/A
Responding to voice mail messages	5	4	3	2	1	N/A
RELIABILITY (Dependable and consistent responses)						
Placing orders in a timely manner	5	4	3	2	1	N/A
Resolving problems	5	4	3	2	1	N/A
Working with you in a cooperative manner	5	4	3	2	1	N/A
JOB KNOWLEDGE (Accurate and skillful responses)						
Answering questions to your satisfaction	5	4	3	2	1	N/A
Recommending other resources for information needs, if necessary	5	4	3	2	1	N/A
Knowledgeable regarding product information	5	4	3	2	1	N/A
Knowledgeable regarding Medicare policies	5	4	3	2	1	N/A
INITIATIVE (Action-oriented responses)						
Offering substitutes (with the exception of nutritional products) if desired product is unavailable	5	4	3	2	1	N/A
Developing solutions to correct recurring problems	5	4	3	2	1	N/A
PROFESSIONALISM						
Displaying mature and appropriate conduct	5	4	3	2	1	N/A

(Please circle one number for each category)

We appreciate any additional comments, concerns, or suggestions you may have!

_____

_____

_____

Please return this form before _____ , by folding to indicate ABC HealthCare's mailing address on the outside and secure with tape. Thank you for your time and feedback! This form will be reviewed and communicated to the employee.

Technical Support Representative Appraisal Questionnaire

This questionnaire is to be done periodically as a measure of performance for the Technical Support Team. Each Technical Support Representative identifies at least two associates with whom they have the most contact at the Division for which he or she is responsible. The Technical Support Manager then contacts the identified associates and surveys them, usually by phone.

Technical Support Representative (subject of appraisal): _____

Division of Responsibility (ex. Southern): _____

Division Associate responding to survey: _____

Interview Conducted by: _____

Date of Interview: _____

Please rank (on a scale of 1-10) the Technical Support Representative for your Division in the following areas:

Availability

_____ When you contact the Technical Support Representative by phone, how often does he or she personally answer the call, i.e., no voice mail?
1 = he or she is almost never personally available to answer
5 = he or she is personally available on half the calls
10 = he or she is always available

_____ When your Technical Support Representative is out of town, does he or she leave instructions on his voice mail or otherwise so you know whom you should contact in his absence?
1 = never
5 = half the time
10 = always

_____ How well does the existing voice mail, fax and paging systems meet your needs for making the necessary communication contacts in a timely fashion?
1 = poorly
5 = adequate or needs slight improvement
10 = superior

Communication/Etiquette

_____ When you speak to your Technical Support Representative, does he or she seem genuinely interested in helping?
1 = low interest in helping
10 = high interest in helping

_____ When you speak to your Technical Support Representative, do you find your representative to be Professional?
1 = no
10 = very professional

_____ How well does your Technical Support Representative listen to your needs?
1 = poorly
10 = very good listener

Responsiveness

_____ How well are you satisfied with the amount of time it takes for your Technical Support Representative to respond to your recorded voice mail or fax message?
1 = very dissatisfied
10 = very satisfied

_____ When your Technical Support Representative has indicated that additional research or investigation is needed to get you an answer, how well are you satisfied with the time it takes to get the final answer?
1 = very dissatisfied
10 = very satisfied

_____ When your Technical Support Representative indicates that he or she will respond by a specified time, does he or she always respond as promised, even if the response is only to inform you that he or she is still seeking an answer?
1 = never
10 = always

Product Knowledge/Problem Solving

_____ How would you rank your Technical Support Representative's personal level of product/process knowledge?
1 = totally inadequate
5 = adequate or needs slight improvement
10 = very superior

_____ When your Technical Support Representative is not personally able to provide an answer immediately, does he or she generally know whom to call to get an answer?
1 = never
5 = half the time
10 = he or she always knows whom to contact for an answer

_____ How would you rank your Technical Support Representative's ability to solve problems using whatever resources are available?
1 = totally inadequate
5 = adequate or needs slight improvement
10 = very superior

General

_____ Does your Technical Support Representative seem to have a good working relationship with other members of the company?
1 = poor relationship
5 = adequate or needs slight improvement
10 = very strong working relationships

_____ How would you rank your Technical Support Representative's overall level of performance?
1 = poor
5 = adequate to needs slight improvement
10 = superior

_____ Does your Technical Support Representative seem to seek continuous improvement in his or her ability to serve you?
1 = no
5 = sometimes
10 = always

Glossary

Cognitive Ties — The logical flow of a questionnaire due to well-developed transitional phrases and proper grouping of questions.

Contact Experience — The experience associated with contacting a company.

Cycle of Service — All the moment of truths that occur during a typical service experience with a company.

Items-in-a-Series — A type of response set that specifically measures attributes using a common rating scale.

Loyalty — The degree to which a customer is willing to continue his or her relationship with a company. This typically is measured by their willingness to repurchase or recommend the company's product or service.

Moment of Truth — A point of contact by a customer with a company where opinions are formed.

Points of Pain — The experiences that a customer has with a company that create customer dissatisfaction and ultimately customer defection.

Population — Customers eligible to participate in a survey because they possess pre-determined characteristics (age, own a certain product, live within the geographical area being studied, etc.).

Pre-coded Questionnaire — A questionnaire that contains tags beside each response to facilitate easier sorting of the responses.

Pre-Testing — Evaluation of a questionnaire prior to conducting the actual survey to ensure that the questionnaire is valid (i.e., the questionnaire is measuring what it was designed to measure).

Respondent — A customer who participates in a survey by responding to questions.

Respondent Drop-Off — A customer's unwillingness to finish completing the questionnaire.

Respondent Fatigue — Frustration, boredom or tiredness experienced by a customer that results in their failure to complete the questionnaire.

Response Set — The answer choices in a questionnaire from which a customer may choose.

Screening — Qualifying customers for a survey according to specific predetermined criteria.

Social Desirability Response Bias — The degree to which a customer's responses are biased by perceived social norms.

Survey — A study conducted to measure the attitudes, beliefs and behaviors of customers.

Top-box Rating — The response that represents the highest score in a range of responses.

Transitional Phrases — Words used to bridge the gap between different sections of a questionnaire.

Questionnaire — A tool used to solicit the perceptions of customers.

Validity — The degree to which the survey measures what it is intended to measure.

References

Books

Anton, Jon, Listening to the voice of the customer: 16 steps to a successful customer measurement program, The Customer Service Group, New York, NY, 1997

Belson, William A., Design and Understanding of Survey Questions, Gower Publishing Ltd., Aldershot, Hants., England, 1981

Berdie, Douglas R. and Anderson, John F., Questionnaires: Design and Use, The Scarecrow Press Inc., Metuchen NJ, 1974

Dillman, Don A., Mail Telephone Surveys: The Total Design Method, John Wiley & Sons, New York, NY, 1978

Hepworth, Michael, Put a Lock on Customer Loyalty: The bottom line benefits of effective customer contact management, Toronto, 1997

Kano, Noriaki and Seraku, N. and Takahashi, F., Attractive Quality and Must-Be Quality Elements, Journal of Japanese Society for Quality Control, Vol.14, #2, 1984.

Lininger, Charles A. and Warwick, Donald P., The Sample Survey: Theory and Practice, McGraw-Hill Book Company, 1975

Mangoine, Thomas W., Mail Surveys: Improving the Quality, Sage Publications, London, 1995

Oppenheim, A.N., Questionnaire Design, Interviewing and Attitude Measurement, Pinter Publishers, London, 1992

Schriesheim, C.A and Denisi, A.S., Item presentation as an influence on questionnaire validity: A Field Experiment, Educational and Psychological Measurement, 40(1), 1980

Sudman, Seymour and Bradburn, Norman M., Improving Interview Method and Questionnaire Design, Jossey-Bass Publishers, San Francisco, CA, 1981

Sudman, Seymour and Bradburn, Norman M., Asking Questions: A Practical Guide to Questionnaire Design, Jossey-Bass Publishers, San Francisco, CA, 1983

Database

Hepworth + Company CustomerPulse™ Database, A collection of over 80 customer satisfaction studies representing more than 65,000 responses internationally.

Web Sites

CyberAtlas (http://www.cyberatlas.com/market/size/how_many_people.html)

InfoPoll (http://www.accesscable.net/~infopoll/resource.htm)

The Business Research Lab (http://busreslab.com/tips/tip17.htm)